Computer-Assisted Instruction in Composition

COMPUTER-ASSISTED INSTRUCTION IN COMPOSITION

CREATE YOUR OWN!

Cynthia L. Selfe
Michigan Technological University, Houghton

Book Design: Tom Kovacs for TGK Design

NCTE Stock Number 08148

Library of Congress Cataloging-in-Publication Data

Selfe, Cynthia L., 1951–
   Computer-assisted instruction in composition.

   1. English language—Composition and exercises—
Study and teaching—Data processing.   2. English
language—Rhetoric—Study and teaching—Data
processing.   3. Computer-assisted instruction.
I. Title.
PE1404.S38   1986   808'.042'0285   86-12340
ISBN 0-8141-0814-8

CONTENTS

Acknowledgments   vii

Introduction   1

1. Identifying Assumptions about Writing and Pedagogy   7
2. Getting Started on a CAI Project   15
3. Working with a Design Team   35
4. Making Pedagogical Decisions about a CAI Lesson   47
5. Integrating Response and Evaluation into a CAI Lesson   75
6. Thinking about Screen Display   99
7. Field Testing a CAI Lesson   121
8. Spreading the Word about CAI Software   139

ACKNOWLEDGMENTS

Writing, for me, has never been an easy task, and I have always been jealous of those colleagues who can say they "love to write," that they get a "sensual pleasure" from putting pen to paper or fingers to keyboards. For me, writing is painful. The only part I like is *having written*. Therefore, it is with the deepest gratitude I acknowledge those intrepid souls who helped me through this book-writing venture.

For the material in this book, I owe the most to those professional colleagues with whom I work every day at Michigan Tech: Billie Wahlstrom, who continues to contribute most of the fresh perspective, insight, and energy that goes into my thinking about work with computers; Tim Nelson, of Michigan Tech Software, who struggled with Billie and me as we learned to produce software by trial and error; Art Young, who knows the magic of collegial support and encouragement; all my humanities colleagues who gave me a home and a family at Michigan Tech; Fred Erbisch and the Creativity Grants Committee, who funded a summer of book writing; Bill Powers, a Dean with a heart and a fondness for electronic composition; and finally, Ruthann Ruehr, Dickie Selfe, and all the STC computer consultants who make the Center for Computer-Assisted Language Instruction the strange and wonderful place that it is.

In addition, this book would be a slim volume indeed without the information and help I have gotten from colleagues at other institutions who are wrestling with the problems and potential that computers have brought to our profession: Hugh Burns, Helen Schwartz, Dawn and Ray Rodrigues, Bill Wresch, Lillian Bridwell and Don Ross, Jim Collins and Elizabeth Sommers, Kate Kiefer, and others far too numerous to identify individually.

And of course, in the beginning and in the end, there is Dickie; together we work at forging a sillier tomorrow.

INTRODUCTION

Some History

There was a time, not too long ago, when English teachers were known for their red pens. They gave assignments, waited a week, and then sat down to highlight in crimson the obvious errors in spelling, logic, and punctuation in students' papers. Not much time was spent thinking about writing as a process. Revision often consisted of having students do "corrections."

We have changed with the times. For most English teachers, the whole idea of composition—including prewriting activities, drafting, and revision—has undergone a radical alteration in the last ten years. The explosion of research on the processes involved in composing, which began in the 1970s, has continued to have a central impact on the teaching of writing wherever it occurs in the English curriculum. Our increased awareness of process has influenced not only the way we teach composition but the way we teach *any* class that involves writing. The result has been an increased work load for all of us. We have found that it takes much longer to work with a student through lengthy prewriting activities and multiple drafts of a paper than it does simply to examine a written product in its final form.

In their war against increasing work loads, English teachers have turned to writing laboratories, professional tutors, and teaching assistants for help. These solutions, however, have often proven to be expensive and, in a period of budget reduction and frozen hiring, unrealistic.

One ally that continues to provide hope for the writing teacher is the computer. While an initial investment in these machines and the software that drives them can be costly, many teachers feel that, over a period of time, computers can serve as effective, efficient teaching tools. Some instructors have discovered, for example, that the relatively simple tasks of teaching grammar and usage are easily adapted to binary logic and that microcomputers can,

for these mechanical tasks, accommodate more students, with more repetitions, than the most patient teachers can. Thus, computer-assisted instruction (CAI) programs such as PLATO, Houghton Mifflin's Dolphin Language Series, and the University of Notre Dame's English Tutorials are able to act effectively as electronic workbooks that teach students how to use commas, avoid dangling modifiers, and recognize the subject of a sentence. These programs free teachers for more difficult tasks in the composition classroom—lecturing, holding individual conferences, or organizing small group work.

A few pioneers have even begun to create a new generation of CAI programs, programs that go beyond drill and practice to deal with matters of process and content. Hugh Burns (1980), for example, has written CAI that provides prewriting or invention stimulus. Using a hypothesis/support focus, Helen Schwartz (1984) has created interactive CAI for use in literature classes. Other efforts include CAI that will help writers compose essays (Wresch 1983), and CAI that combines word-processing functions and programs for invention and revision (Von Blum and Cohen 1984).

What Can Computers and CAI Do?

What can English teachers expect of computers and the new generation of CAI? Although computers, even with the best software, are still unable to understand text, to make sense out of paragraphs, or words, they *can* do certain tasks very well. The new generation of CAI will take advantage of the following capabilities:

Recognizing

Many people talk about computers "reading" things; it may be more accurate, however, to say that they can—again with the help of appropriate software—"recognize" patterns or arrangements of letters. Thus, computers can recognize and point out a particular word, phrase, or sentence when it is used in a student paper; identify marks of punctuation; find the occurrences of various linguistic features in any given text, and identify names or numbers. Computers can, with their recognizing skill, search for a particular item in a long text and evaluate whether the item matches a preset response or list of responses made up by a writing teacher.

Counting

Given the right kinds of directions, computers can also count everything they can recognize. They can count and calculate, for instance, the average number of letters per word, the average number of words in a theme, or the average length of sentences in any given text. Computers can count, among other things, the nouns, prepositions, and verbs for syntactic or stylistic analyses; they can tally the right and wrong answers for testing situations; they can keep track of the occurrences of a specific phrase or clause in a paragraph; or they can count the number of entries in a bibliography.

Storing and Record Keeping

In addition to recognizing and counting, computers can store information and keep records. Appropriate software can, for example, direct computers to record the specific responses students make to a writing activity or question; store freewrites, audience analyses, and journal entries; keep drafts or parts of drafts; and save demographic information or grading information about students, classes, or groups. This information can then be called up and revised by the teacher or by a student.

Branching

With the right software, a computer can allow students to follow various branches of a program. As a result, computers can offer a wide choice of different paths through a writing-intensive exercise, provide individualized instruction according to students' previous performances, or vary responses according to whether students provide appropriate or inappropriate answers.

Evaluating

Because computers can recognize certain patterns and store information, with the help of intelligent software

they can also evaluate responses by matching key words or phrases against a preset list of appropriate or inappropriate answers made up by a teacher.

Keeping Time

Most computers now have internal clocks that allow them to time writing exercises or journal writing episodes, keep track of how long students spend on a particular activity, and print records of the time students spend on computer-assisted lessons.

In addition to these capabilities, computers and CAI have advantages over human teachers in certain educational settings for the following reasons:

Repetition

Some educators maintain that computers, because they are machines, are inherently inferior to humans as teachers. But because computers *are* machines, they will, given the appropriate software, repeat lessons, concepts, and directions ad infinitum and never experience the boredom, frustration, or exhaustion of overworked human teachers.

Adaptability

Computers also have the advantage of changing content specialty with the software they use. Thus, the same machine, using CAI written by several different human experts, can act as a linguistics teacher, literature tutor, reading instructor, and composition specialist. In certain educational settings, where full-time human specialists are not available, a computer, with the right software, can teach courses that otherwise could not be offered.

Consistency

Once software programs are written, field tested, revised, and perfected by an author/teacher, they can be run again and again on a computer, providing a consistent and systematic program of instruction that will cover the same key concepts for every user.

Availability

Computers, and the CAI programs they run, can be made available for instructional purposes twenty-four hours each day. Students who cannot match their schedules with those of human educators can have access to mechanical teachers whenever they require help.

What Can't Computers and CAI Do?

Despite the capabilities of computers, and CAI, machines still have some distinct limitations when compared to human teachers, especially when it comes to teaching writing. Understanding these limitations may help people avoid frustration when they use computers.

Limitations of Intelligence

Although computer technology has made amazing strides in the area of artificial intelligence during the last several years, computers still cannot "understand" even the simplest text as humans can. The human brain learns to "know" words in a rich contextual fabric of experience and associations, and, as yet, programmers have not been entirely successful in simulating this kind of knowledge for computers. Thus, although there are sophisticated programs that allow computers to perform certain linguistic and logical tasks, computers cannot read a student's paper and understand content, analyze logical structures, or comment specifically on paragraph development in the same way that human teachers consistently and effectively can.

Response Limitations

Computers are also limited in their responses to student writing. Unlike humans, computers cannot modify their responses according to students' moods, the interest they display in a subject, their body language, or any other of the important considerations that shape human communication in a conversational situation. Programmers and authors, in their attempts to duplicate human response patterns, can only anticipate a limited number of answers that users might give to certain questions or situations and then designate the response that computers are to make for each such answer. Because the number of answers to any given question or situation is so large, inappropriate computer responses often result.

Programming Limitations

As an educational tool, computers are also limited by the imagination and the expertise of the programmers and authors who code and write software. Like any medium, CAI must be pedagogically sound if it is to be valuable in the classroom, taking into account individual learning styles, cognitive strategies, and lan-

guage skills. In addition, if CAI is to be useful in writing courses, it must be theoretically sound as well, emphasizing rhetorical principles, composing processes, and the close relationship between reading and writing.

Perhaps the most important limitation of computers and CAI has to do with the inherent limitations of the computer programming operation. Computer programs are often written by people who are more concerned with producing marketable software than producing CAI that is pedagogically and theoretically sound. There are very few software designers who have extensive educational training or teaching experience, and even fewer who have training in composition or rhetoric.

Computers in the Writing Classroom

With the increasing emphasis on process-based composition instruction during the last decade, the burden on writing teachers has increased dramatically. Teachers who guide students through a series of increasingly refined drafts of a paper and offer comprehensive feedback for each of these drafts are seeking ways of lightening their work load.

Computers can offer help in teaching composition. Along with appropriate instructional programs which tell the machine how to recognize answers, store information, count items, branch, evaluate, and keep time, computers can teach a wide range of composition skills, concepts, and heuristics. In addition, such instruction has the added advantage of being available for endless repetitions of the same material.

Some experts point out that computers are limited in the way they can respond to students' input and, thus, limited in their usefulness in the composition classroom. But most of those same experts would agree that computers and good CAI—CAI that is both pedagogically and theoretically sound—have the potential for assuming the more repetitious tasks of composition instruction and for freeing the teacher to address the creative problems that require a human instructor.

Why Write Your Own CAI?

A quick look at the latest composition journal or a tour of the exhibits at a national conference on composition will reveal a plethora of CAI programs that claim to be designed for the writing classroom.

Unfortunately, too few CAI programs offer much beyond electronic workbook material. In general, CAI designed for the writing classroom suffers from two significant shortcomings. First, such CAI has, in most cases, simply duplicated the programmed, audiovisual materials developed for slides, tapes, and filmstrips over a decade ago. CAI authors are only now beginning to take advantage of the branching or interactive capabilities of new hardware and software. Second, much of the CAI currently available to composition teachers focuses only on the surface features of text or on editing and proofreading, two relatively minor activities within the larger process of composing. It is very difficult to find commercial CAI that addresses larger rhetorical issues or the entire spectrum of activities involved in the composing process—from the first planning efforts, through the writing of multiple drafts, to the final revision and editing activities. A few pioneers such as Hugh Burns, Helen Schwartz at Oakland University, the WANDAH (a.k.a. HBJ Writer) team at the University of California, Los Angeles, and William Wresch of the University of Wisconsin–Marinette have been able to apply the computer to more complex matters of process and content in composition classrooms; nevertheless, their work is the exception rather than the rule.

The most obvious reason for the simplistic CAI now available to composition teachers involves the fundamental schism existing between the humanities and technical fields. Although both teachers and computer technicians have turned their attention toward software design, they have not yet discovered how to work together. Much of the CAI currently on the market for composition classrooms has been written by English teachers who have only a limited grasp of current techniques of software design, or by technicians from computer software companies who have only a limited vision of modern composition theory and pedagogy. The result of this schism is software limited in its usefulness.

This book describes a process of creating CAI lessons for the composition classroom that has grown out of our CAI experiences at Michigan Technological University. It has been tested and modified in workshops with teachers of English at the elementary, secondary, and college levels. This process results in CAI that evolves organically from the set of theoretical principles, both rhetorical and pedagogical, that underlie a writing program. This process uses the talents of both composition specialists and computer scientists in a cooperative, team effort. Using the team approach allows composition teachers to generate CAI that is both rhetorically sound and technically sophisticated.

Suggestions for Using This Book

At this point, we would like to offer readers some suggestions for using this text. In the following chapters, the steps for creating successful CAI are arranged in a progressive sequence that approximates the process of software design. However, because the printed page has only two dimensions, we cannot present, at one time, all the information CAI authors will need. When, for instance, in the second chapter, we suggest that authors start writing a screen-by-screen script of a CAI lesson, it would also be ideal if we could, simultaneously, present them with all the information in the subsequent three chapters as well, information about lesson design, screen design, and evaluation that will necessarily shape the scripts they create.

In the traditional print format this book depends on, however, such a simultaneous presentation is impossible. We can only attempt to minimize the problems readers might encounter with this linear presentation by providing the following suggestions for using this book.

1. First, read the Introduction to get an idea of the book's content and organization.

2. Next, read the material presented in Chapters One through Seven; don't worry about completing the worksheets. Rather concentrate on surveying and understanding the information contained in each step.

3. After reading through the text the first time, go back and review each chapter carefully, this time completing the worksheets at the end of each section. Refer to various parts of the book as needed, but complete the design tasks in the order they are presented.

4. Finally, allow for the luxury of revision. You might get halfway through the design process described in this book before you discover the CAI lesson on which you really want to work or before you realize that your lesson will require major revision if it is to succeed in your classroom. Don't get discouraged. Such realizations are characteristic of design, problem-solving, *and* writing processes. Very few authors will be able to go through the entire process without making substantial revisions of their initial ideas about a CAI lesson.

Overview of the Book

This book describes a process of creating CAI for the composition classroom. It begins with an examination of the theoretical principles underlying a composition course or program and moves toward an increasingly refined instructional product. For the purposes of our discussion, each of the chapters in this book will describe one part or step of the process. The process itself, however, like any problem-solving process, is both complex and recursive and must be modified freely to work successfully within a specific writing program.

Identifying Assumptions about Writing and Pedagogy

If CAI is to be useful in a writing program, it must be informed by the same theoretical assumptions that underlie the teaching within this program. Chapter One discusses the importance of identifying assumptions about writing and the teaching of writing, and of using these assumptions to shape CAI projects.

Getting Started on a CAI Project

Chapter Two describes how to get started on a CAI project by choosing a suitable topic, analyzing this topic in terms of teaching tasks, defining how the proposed instructional unit would fit into a writing classroom or program, sketching an initial overview of the instruction, and starting to write a screen-by-screen script of the instruction.

Working with a Design Team

Chapter Three discusses how to work with a design team to create CAI software for a writing-intensive classroom or program. Combining the expertise of specialists in composition, computer technology, education, and marketing in a cooperative venture can produce valuable CAI that is sound in both content and structure.

Making Pedagogical Decisions about a CAI Lesson

In the initial stages of a CAI project, certain pedagogical decisions must be made. Authors, for instance, will want to identify the instructional objectives that form the basis for the CAI, consider the screen and frame types that will be employed to convey the instruction, and think about the lesson design and

approach used to structure the lesson. Chapter Four discusses the choices to be made in each of these areas.

Integrating Response and Evaluation into a CAI Lesson

Writing CAI also involves making decisions about how to respond to the material that students type on the computer screen. These decisions involve considering how, when, where, or if student answers should be evaluated; whether student answers and student writing should be stored; and who should have access to the storage files.

Thinking about Screen Display

Designing the screen presentation of instructional material involves making choices about functional areas, print fonts, graphics, color, highlighting, and other special effects. Chapter Six discusses the issues surrounding such choices.

Field Testing a CAI Lesson

Much of the real work on a CAI unit must begin only after it is field tested on a targeted student audience. Field tests may involve working with various team members, administrators, students, and other teachers. Chapter Seven describes how to set up and implement field-testing situations.

Spreading the Word about CAI Software

Often, the success of a CAI project depends on communication with colleagues. Chapter Eight discusses how to talk about CAI projects to teachers who don't use computers as a tool in their writing classes and how to find other teachers who are engaged in their own CAI projects.

Sources Cited

Burns, Hugh L., and G. H. Culp. 1980. Simulating Invention in English Composition through Computer-Assisted Instruction. *Educational Technology* 20 (8):5–10.

Schwartz, Helen J. 1984. Teaching Writing with Computer Aids. *College English* 46 (3):239–47.

Von Blum, R., and M. E. Cohen. 1984. "WANDAH: Writing Aid and Author's Helper." In *The Com-*

puter in Composition Instruction, ed. William Wresch. 154–73. Urbana, Ill.: National Council of Teachers of English.

Wresch, William. 1983. Computer Essay Generation. *The Computing Teacher* 11(3): 63–65.

1 IDENTIFYING ASSUMPTIONS ABOUT WRITING AND PEDAGOGY

The process of creating CAI, as it is described in this book, involves a team of experts working together to take advantage of their combined specialities. The success of any CAI destined for the composition classroom, however, will ultimately depend on you, the writing teacher. Only you can make informed decisions about how, or indeed if, computer-assisted instruction can help you teach students; where it could fit into your program or your class; which needs it could address; when such instruction would be beneficial; and what content material it is best suited to communicate. And, only you can write the initial scripts for the CAI, scripts that tell the computer programmer or software designer what you want the computer to do.

Before these decisions can be made, however, and before a team can begin to create a successful piece of CAI, the composition teacher must answer the following questions:

1. What are my students' writing problems?
2. What are my assumptions about writing and composing?
3. What are my assumptions about the way writing should be taught?

This chapter discusses the need to address these questions before beginning to create a CAI lesson and provides a systematic way of doing so. In a pattern we try to follow throughout this book, we have also provided sample answers produced by an imaginary teacher, named Jean, who teaches first-year composition at a small, four-year college. In fact, Jean's answers are compiled from the answers of teachers who have responded to these activities in actual workshops we have given on creating CAI.

At the end of the chapter, you will be asked to answer each of the questions yourself on a worksheet we provide.

What Are My Students' Writing Problems?

The profession continues to learn how to teach writing more effectively. Research and scholarship during the last decade indicate the importance of approaching writing as a process; of identifying audience and purpose in rhetorical situations; of providing both evaluative and personal feedback to writers; of recognizing the essential connections among writing, reading, listening, and speaking. Rather than bring computers into our classroom because we are enamored of them as electronic gadgets, we should use computers and computer-assisted instruction because they can help us teach students these very important concepts and do so in a way that complements our own teaching. CAI, in other words, like any type of writing instruction, should help us address the specific problems that our students exhibit when they compose.

One good way of making sure that CAI relates directly to an assessment of student needs involves identifying those needs. For most teachers, this task is second nature. In fact, most of our pedagogical practices and theoretical assumptions in the writing classroom grow directly out of the observations we make of student needs. We watch our students, we see how they write and from what writing problems they suffer, and we draw certain conclusions. With each student we help, these conclusions become stronger, more certain, and our practices are modified.[1] Here is a list of student writing problems that Jean might have compiled after observing her own students.

Example of Identifying Student Writing Problems

Process Problems
invention
planning
getting started
revising in multiple drafts
editing

Attitude problems
commitment to writing
fear/apprehension
understanding importance of writing in career
refusal to make multiple revisions

Mechanical Problems
parallelism
agreement
attribution
spelling
sexist language

Logic Problems
organizing paragraphs
organizing essays
development
general vs. specific
topic sentences

You probably noticed that Jean clustered her students' writing problems into easily recognizable groups. This categorization will make her task easier when she has to decide which problem area she wants to address in her first CAI lesson. You might also note that Jean was as specific as possible in identifying her students' writing problems, a characteristic that will, at a later point, help her focus the CAI lesson that she wants to create.

At the end of this chapter, on Worksheet 1: Identifying Student Writing Problems, you will be asked to list those writing problems your students exhibit in much the same way that Jean did. Remember, this is a brainstorming task, so identify as many problems as possible and be as specific as possible in your listing. You can turn to that worksheet now and complete the listing task, or you can read the rest of this chapter and finish the worksheet later.

What Are My Assumptions about Writing and Composing?

All teachers—through experience, observations, and reading—have amassed a list of theoretical premises that inform their teaching of writing. A teacher might believe, for instance, that writing involves a problem-solving *process* as well as an end *product,* or that all authors can benefit from feedback as they work through the writing process. Teachers test and modify these premises continually; each student and each

writing-intensive class provides data that support the assumptions or that indicate a need for modification.

These same premises can serve to shape CAI software. In fact, if these premises are identified and used to determine the content and approach of a piece of CAI, the specific goals of the software will closely match the goals of writing instruction in general and assure a cohesive approach to teaching writing. Authors who fail to identify their assumptions about writing before they design software run the risk of producing materials that are philosophically unrelated to the rest of their instructional activities.

Following, as an example, you'll see a list of assumptions about writing that might have been compiled by Jean, as she thought about the kind of CAI lesson she would like to design. Examine the list, and see if you have any theoretical premises in common.

Example of Identifying Assumptions about Writing

1. Writing involves a complex process of planning, drafting, revising, and editing activities that occur in dynamically recursive patterns.

2. Writing to learn (expressive writing, journal writing, freewriting) is fundamentally different than writing to communicate.

3. The development of writing skills is determined by the developmental process of human learning.

4. Writing, because it involves crystallizing thought into linguistic symbols, necessarily involves learning and thinking.

5. Everyone has a different set of writing problems.

6. Different writing purposes (to persuade, to inform, to express, to amuse) and different writing modes (narration, description, classification, etc.) involve different challenges, skills, and activities for students.

7. Writing and reading are more than complementary skills; they are integrally connected at the most basic physical and cognitive levels.

You probably noted that the assumptions Jean listed about writing are stated in quite general terms and follow no particular pattern of rank or logic. In fact, Jean was asked to take only five or ten minutes for this brainstorming task and encouraged to record those assumptions that came immediately to mind when she thought about writing. Later in this chapter, you'll be asked to compile a similar list.

What Are My Assumptions about Teaching Writing?

The observations teachers make of students' writing problems shape not only their assumptions about the act of writing, but also their assumptions about teaching writing. And these assumptions about the teaching of writing, in turn, determine the type of instruction that goes on within a writing classroom or program. For example, if a teacher assumes that writing involves a process as well as a final product and she sees her students having trouble with various parts of that process (invention, for instance, or revising a preliminary draft), then she will teach students process-oriented strategies for solving writing problems. If a teacher believes that all authors can benefit from feedback as they engage in writing problems and she notes that her students have problems shaping their texts to a reader's needs, she might incorporate peer-audience feedback into her writing classes.

These assumptions about how writing should be taught should also determine the kind of CAI software that is used in the composition classroom. An example will illustrate the importance of this point. One teacher we know got a $5,000 grant to spend two months of her summer vacation writing a short CAI lesson on writing expository essays. She planned the lesson for use by all the teachers in her high school's writing program for college-bound seniors. Unfortunately, before creating the lesson, she failed to identify the assumptions about teaching writing that her colleagues in this program shared. The following year, to her dismay, the CAI gathered dust on the school library's shelf and was seldom checked out by her fellow teachers for their classes. They found the program, which stressed a rigidly prescriptive approach to style, to be of little use in their classes that, instead, emphasized style as an organic outgrowth of the communication situation.

At the end of this chapter, on Worksheet 3: Identifying Assumptions about Teaching Writing, you will be asked to take a few minutes to brainstorm and compile a list of your assumptions about teaching writing. In the list that follows, you see what Jean might have compiled in response to the same task.

Example of Identifying Assumptions about Teaching Writing

1. Students must practice writing often if they are to become better writers.
2. Students must practice writing for different purposes and different audiences, and using different modes. Students must be taught strategies for coping with different writing situations.
3. Students must be guided through the process of writing and taught specific strategies for use at various points of this process.
4. Students must receive critical feedback from readers (both peers and teachers) at all stages of the writing process.
5. Students must learn to read critically their own writing and the writing of others—always with an eye toward revision.
6. Students must be given instructional help and practice in mastering their own unique writing problems in the context of real writing tasks.
7. Students must be given sufficient time to practice writing and rewriting.
8. Students must be given chances to succeed in writing situations, even if this means continued rewriting efforts.
9. Students should also be shown how other writers, both professional and amateur, solve writing problems.

You probably noticed that the pedagogical assumptions Jean listed in this example are related directly to her students' writing problems and her assumptions about teaching writing. This consistency makes sense; Jean's observations of students' writing problems, along with her own experiences as a writer, serve to shape her beliefs about writing and about how best to teach writing. When you complete Worksheet 1: Identifying Students' Writing Problems, Worksheet 2: Identifying Assumptions about Writing, and Worksheet 3: Identifying Assumptions about Teaching Writing at the end of this chapter, check to see how consistent your own teaching methods are in relation to the problems your students exhibit as they compose and the assumptions you hold with regard to writing.

Summary

Answering the questions in this chapter is no easy task, but if you pause to think about them now, you may solve some of the problems involved in writing CAI lessons before you even start. Like any instruction that is ultimately successful, CAI must, in both conception and practice, grow organically from the ideas and activities of individual teachers who have developed, tested, and refined their techniques in actual writing classrooms. The tasks outlined in this chapter will help you create this type of successful CAI.

How should you answer the questions we have posed in this chapter? If you plan to write CAI lessons by yourself and for your own classroom, you may simply want to sit down and examine your own rhetorical and pedagogical assumptions—those that are manifested in the writing instruction you give in your classes.

If, however, you are creating CAI that will be useful to a number of teachers in a writing program, you might want to work with that group to answer the questions. This approach will be especially useful if the teachers in your writing program operate their classes on the basis of a common set of theoretical premises (e.g., writing involves a complex process, or writing involves learning and thinking) or if they have identified certain teaching practices (e.g., using peer groups to provide reader feedback, or demanding multiple drafts of a single paper). In such cases, you might find it more valuable to come up with a set of group answers to the three questions we have posed in this chapter.

The worksheets that follow have been provided for you as places to answer the questions from this chapter. Use them to examine your own theoretical and pedagogical assumptions or as a place to identify group assumptions.

Note

1. This particular activity is taken directly from the writing-across-the-curriculum workshops given by faculty at Michigan Technological University. That it is as readily applicable in workshops on CAI as it is in workshops on discipline-based composition illustrates the importance of forming all writing programs around the needs of writers.

Worksheet 1: Identifying Student Writing Problems

Take five or ten minutes to brainstorm, and list below the writing problems you see your students exhibiting. Be as specific as possible.

Now, take the problems you have identified, and organize them into clusters that represent problem *areas*. List these clusters below.

Cluster 1 _____   Cluster 2 _____

Cluster 3 _____   Cluster 4 _____

Cluster 5 _____   Cluster 6 _____

Worksheet 2: Identifying Assumptions about Writing

In the space below, brainstorm for ten or fifteen minutes, and list those assumptions about rhetoric and composition that inform your teaching of writing.

Worksheet 3: Identifying Assumptions about Teaching Writing

In the space below, take ten or twenty minutes to brainstorm, and list the assumptions you make about pedagogy that affect the way you teach in your composition classroom or program.

2 GETTING STARTED ON A CAI PROJECT

The Introduction discussed in a general way what tasks computers can do for us and what things we are better off doing for ourselves. In the last chapter, you listed some of the specific problems your students encounter when they write and some of the premises (about writing and the teaching of writing) upon which your composition program is based. Now, you are ready to begin thinking about the specific kind of CAI project that you want to undertake. In this chapter, we will suggest a series of seven predesign tasks you may complete to help ensure the success of a CAI lesson. These tasks are listed here.

1. Choose a topic to address in a CAI lesson.
2. Adjust the focus of the CAI lesson.
3. Complete a task analysis of the lesson.
4. Examine the lesson in light of assumptions about writing and pedagogy.
5. Determine how the CAI lesson would fit into the current writing program.
6. Create a lesson-overview flow chart.
7. Begin writing a script for the CAI lesson.

1. Choosing a Topic to Address in a CAI Lesson

One of the first tasks to complete when starting work on a CAI lesson involves choosing a topic or a problem area around which to focus the instruction. You identified in Chapter One a list of problems that your students exhibit when they write (Worksheet 1: Identifying Student Writing Problems). This list will make an excellent starting point for identifying a lesson's content, especially if you begin by arranging your students' writing problems according to some sort of priority. In the following example, you'll note how Jean, our representative teacher, might have taken her original listing and ranked the problem areas she identified from 1 ("Deal with these now!") to 4 ("Deal with these later").

Example of Ranking of Student Writing Problems

2nd Priority
Process Problems
invention
planning
getting started
revising in multiple drafts
editing

1st Priority
Attitude Problems
commitment to writing
fear/apprehension
understanding importance of writing as a career
refusal to write multiple revisions

4th Priority
Mechanical Problems
parallelism
agreement
attribution
spelling
sexist language

3rd Priority
Logic Problems
organizing papers/paragraphs
development
general vs. specific
topic sentences

In ranking these problems as she did, Jean acted on a belief that "an attitude change" had to precede any positive action on other problems. Also note that she thought the students' problems with the writing process should receive particular emphasis in her classroom. After completing this ranking exercise, Jean might decide she should write a CAI lesson that addressed some of her students' prewriting problems: getting started and invention.

On Worksheet 4: Ranking Students' Writing Problems we will ask you to make a similar ranking of the problem areas you identified earlier, keeping in mind the order of their instructional priorities in your classroom or writing program. This ranking should provide you with a general idea of a topic area for your own CAI lesson. You may turn to this worksheet now and complete this task, or finish reading this chapter first to get an overview of the six remaining predesign tasks.

2. Adjusting the Focus of the CAI Lesson

Once you have ranked the writing problems your students encounter and chosen one topic or problem around which to build a lesson, you can take time to decide how to focus this instruction. How much of the problem can you tackle effectively in one CAI lesson? What part of the problem is most important to teach your students? Of course, your response to this problem will depend on your own teaching situation. If, for example, you are teaching writing in an elementary school, you might need to choose one part of a writing problem that could be addressed in a CAI lesson lasting between five and fifteen minutes, one that would keep the interest of younger students. If, on the other hand, you are teaching a technical writing class at a community college, you might want to design a CAI lesson around a more complex topic that might last forty-five minutes or even longer.

It is difficult to make these decisions if you have had limited chances to try out commercial or homemade CAI lessons written expressly for students like those you teach. How big a topic is too big? How little a topic is too little? A sound practice in this case is to draw a diagram that will illustrate your topic on several different levels of generality, each level representing the content of a different CAI lesson. Figure 2.1 shows how Jean might have represented the CAI lesson addressing her students' prewriting problems.

You'll notice that Jean can now use this diagram to adjust her approach to her planned CAI lesson. She can, for example, start working on the medium-

sized lesson she identified, entitled "Generating Ideas," which might cover the concepts of brainstorming, diagraming, freewriting, imagining, and listing. If, however, Jean finds this lesson too large or too time-consuming for the students she teaches, she could move down a level on her diagram and address prewriting techniques on a more limited level by focusing on freewriting as a specific strategy.

At the end of this chapter, we have provided an activity, Worksheet 5: Adjusting the Focus of a CAI Lesson, on which you may create a similar diagram for the topic or writing problem you have chosen. You may turn to this worksheet now and begin this activity, or you may read the remainder of this chapter first. You might want to draw several such diagrams if you have not made a final decision about the topic on which you would like to concentrate.

3. Completing a Task Analysis of the CAI Lesson

Before you actually try this next task, you should complete two important activities: first, choose one topic or problem you would like to address in a CAI lesson, and second, using the method we explained in the last predesign task, select a realistic focus for this lesson. If you're still not sure how big your CAI lesson should be, we suggest starting at the most specific level of your diagram. Working on a lesson with a specific and limited focus is extremely important if you are creating your first CAI lesson. By creating a small, focused instructional packet, you can gauge the effort and time required for CAI projects without making too large an investment of energy.

Up until this point in the process of creating a CAI lesson, it is easy, as an author, to think very generally about the topic you have chosen to address. The time comes, however, when it is necessary to identify the specific concepts or activities you will include in your lesson. For the next exercise, we will ask you to do a task analysis of the instruction involved in the CAI lesson you are planning, and to anticipate the concepts

Example of Adjusting the Focus of a CAI Lesson

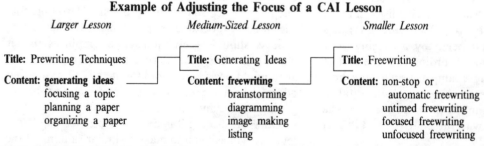

Larger Lesson   *Medium-Sized Lesson*   *Smaller Lesson*

Title: Prewriting Techniques   **Title:** Generating Ideas   **Title:** Freewriting

Content: generating ideas ——   **Content: freewriting** ——   **Content:** non-stop or
    focusing a topic   brainstorming   automatic freewriting
    planning a paper   diagramming   untimed freewriting
    organizing a paper   image making   focused freewriting
                listing   unfocused freewriting

Figure 2.1: Sample of Worksheet 5 Activity

and activities that will be a part of the lesson. To make this task easier, picture the activities you would use to explain the lesson's central concepts in a traditional classroom setting. What concepts would you explain? What intermediate learning steps would you plan for students who want to master the concepts you've identified as part of the lesson?

In the following list you'll find a task analysis that Jean might have done for her CAI lesson on freewriting.

Example of Completing a Task Analysis of a CAI Lesson

Freewriting
purpose of freewriting
timed or automatic freewriting
untimed freewriting
focused freewriting
keeping a journal

If, in this exercise, you simply list those concepts and activities that you *always* cover in connection with a specific topic when teaching a writing course, you will find this task to be relatively simple. Indeed, the list above represents five concepts and activities that Jean might explain or use in a class *whenever* she introduces the topic of freewriting as a prewriting activity—whether or not she chooses to use the computer as a teaching tool. Because the task-analysis list is a description of the writing activities you have developed and tested as a part of actual instructional sequences, it can, when complete, serve as a valuable and realistic outline of the CAI lesson you want to create.

At the end of this chapter, on Worksheet 6: Completing a Task Analysis of a CAI Lesson, you will be asked to compile a similar list for the CAI lesson on which you want to work. On a very practical basis, this worksheet will help you estimate the size of the lesson to be planned. You may, after completing this listing, decide that it would be advantageous to attack the topic on a more limited level. You may turn now to Worksheet 6 and complete the task analysis, or you may finish reading this chapter for an overview of the four remaining predesign tasks before beginning the worksheet.

4. Examining the Lesson in Light of Assumptions about Writing and Pedagogy

In Chapter Two, we talked about the rhetorical and pedagogical assumptions that form the bases for your writing program. We also expressed our belief that any successful CAI would have to address these assumptions. After all, if a CAI lesson doesn't fit smoothly into your existing writing program or match your teaching practices, of what use can it possibly be in your classroom?

To determine where a proposed CAI lesson fits into a writing program and to identify how closely it adheres to the teaching practices already established as a part of an instructional routine, an author must look at the context in which the proposed lesson will be used. Below, we have shown how Jean might have answered some questions that address such contextual concerns. In this activity, Jean would think about how her CAI lesson on freewriting would be affected by the rhetorical and pedagogical assumptions she identified on the worksheets at the end of the first chapter.

Example of Determining the Context for a CAI Lesson

Purpose of Lesson
I want this lesson to teach students how to use several different freewriting strategies effectively. The lesson should also help students understand that freewriting activities will help them generate, develop, and explore their ideas before drafting.

CAI Lesson and Assumptions about Writing
1. Writing involves a complex process.

   Comments: Freewriting, as a prewriting technique, will help show students that writing does not necessarily begin with a full-scale draft. This lesson should be designed to show freewriting as part of a process that involves thinking and explaining even before a first draft is begun.

2. Writing to learn is different from writing to communicate.

   Comments: In this lesson, the purpose of freewriting as a technique of learning and thinking should be stressed. Also, the difference between formal transactional writing, used to communicate to others, and informal expressive writing, used to learn and discover, should be stressed.

3. Writing involves thinking and learning.

   Comments: This lesson should prove to students that they can use writing to find out what they think or remember. Students will see that previously vague or unarticulated thoughts, perhaps those that were only shadows in long-term memory, can be crystallized through writing.

*CAI Lesson and Assumptions about
Teaching Writing*

1. Students must practice writing often if they are
   to become better writers.

   Comments: Students learn to write by practicing writing. This lesson should require students
   to practice freewriting on the computer. It won't
   just *tell* them to freewrite; it will *show* them
   how to freewrite and let them *practice* freewriting on various topics.

2. Students must practice writing for different
   purposes and audiences.

   Comments: In this lesson, students will write
   for the purpose of learning and discovery. They
   will also practice writing to themselves as an
   audience.

3. Students must be guided through the process of
   writing.

   Comments: This lesson will demonstrate freewriting techniques students can use during the
   prewriting stage of their composing process.

As you can see from the example, the purpose of
this activity is to take the assumptions about writing
(identified on Worksheet 2) and the assumptions
about teaching writing (identified on Worksheet 3)
and use them to inform the concept and the content
of the CAI lesson you want to create. If, for instance,
like Jean, you believe that writing involves a complex
process *and* that writing teachers should guide students through this process, you will want to think
carefully about how to design a CAI lesson that leads
students deliberately through a series of process-based
activities on the writing topic you have chosen. At the
end of this chapter, on Worksheet 7: Determining the
Context for a CAI Lesson, you will be asked to make
notes about the impact your own assumptions about
writing and teaching writing will have on the CAI
lesson you want to create. You may turn to this worksheet now and begin this activity or finish reading
about the remaining three predesign tasks first.

5. Fitting the CAI Lesson into a Writing Program

We have just discussed how important it is for the
concept and the content of a CAI lesson to match the
assumptions about writing and teaching that form the
basis for a given composition classroom or program.
In addition, however, it is the composition teacher's
job to define how the students' actual use of the CAI

material will fit into the instructional sequence. Only
the classroom teacher, for example, can determine
whether the CAI lesson should be used outside regular
classroom hours; in what room, what building, what
library the materials might be located to ensure maximum use by students; and if the materials will need
to be documented or explained before students are
asked to use them. In the list below, we have shown
how Jean might address a similar set of concerns.

Example of Fitting CAI into the Writing
Classroom/Program

1. *When will students use the CAI lesson? At what
   point during my instructional sequence do I
   expect them to use the lesson?*

   I'd want them to have used the freewriting lesson
   some time before they began to write their first
   paper of the term--maybe the first week or so.

2. *Where will my students use the CAI lesson?*

   Since the Writing Lab down the hall is open
   from 8 a.m. to 5 p.m., I'll write the CAI lesson
   for their microcomputers (Apples). We also have
   some Apples in the library, which stays open
   even later. I'll make a copy of it so that students
   can use it there too.

3. *How long will students need to spend on the
   CAI lesson? Will this time be a supplement to
   or a substitute for regular classroom instruction?*

   I don't want the kids to spend *more* than one
   hour or *less* than a half an hour learning about
   freewriting. So I have those limits on the lesson.
   I'll assign this CAI as homework—to be done
   any time outside of regular class hours. The
   lesson should allow me to skip the lectures and
   activities on freewriting that I usually have to
   do during the first week of class.

4. *Does the CAI need to be documented or explained before the students use it? Are any supplemental reading or writing materials needed?*

   Well, there are tutors in the lab, but I'm sure
   they won't want to be answering the same questions about how to get started over and over
   again. I'd better write an instruction sheet to
   accompany the CAI. Actually, the instruction
   sheet should only tell users how to turn the
   machine on and put the diskettes in. The rest of
   the instructions should be included in the lesson
   itself. All reading and writing during the lesson
   will be done on the computer screen or with the
   computer keyboard, and students can get a hard

copy of what they did on the printer. As a result, no additional materials will be needed.

At the end of this chapter, on Worksheet 8: Fitting CAI into the Writing Classroom/Program, you will be invited to answer these same questions about how a CAI lesson will "fit" into your writing program. You may turn to that worksheet now and complete it, or you may finish reading about the two remaining predesign steps first.

6. Creating a Lesson-Overview Flowchart for the CAI Instruction

Most English teachers have had little experience with those tools of a programmer's trade called *flowcharts*. However, as the composition specialist on your software design team, you will need some vehicle for explaining your ideas to other team members. Flowcharts, if they're simple and easy to understand, can be one way of bridging the gap between your initial ideas and the team's final execution of the CAI project. So, put your worries aside. The next section describes a system of flowcharting that every teacher can understand.

You might have noticed that Jean responded to these questions as a teacher who was planning to develop a CAI lesson for use in her own writing classes; thus, she had only herself to consult. If you are developing CAI for use by several teachers, however, you may have to come to some sort of consensus on a set of group answers with your fellow teachers to ensure that the CAI lesson you are planning will be a valuable component of your larger writing program.

If you have ever used an outline as an organizing aid while drafting a paper, you already know the value of flowcharts; they help an author visualize the larger structure or framework of a writing project. Although some of the more complex flowcharts that software designers create look like hopeless mazes of geometric figures, a simplified form of such diagrams can be very helpful in representing a general overview of an entire CAI lesson. Hereafter, we will refer to this special kind of flowchart as a *lesson-overview flowchart* because it provides a picture of the entire lesson without going into much detail.

Essentially, the lesson-overview flowchart we will ask you to draw in this chapter will be composed of only three kinds of building blocks.

Ovals. Called a *terminal* or *connector* symbol, an oval marks the beginning of a lesson, the end of a lesson, or a jump to another point in the structure of the lesson.

Rectangles. Called an *operations* box, a rectangle represents one segment or part of your lesson. Rectangles can represent sequences of instruction, writing practice, or skill exercises.

Diamonds. Called *decision* boxes, diamonds represent a branching of the lesson flow, a point of evaluation where you decide in which direction the student or the instruction should go.

In figure 2.2, you can see a sample lesson-overview flowchart that Jean might have made from the task-analysis list she identified on Worksheet 6: Completing a Task Analysis of a CAI Lesson.

You'll notice on this lesson-overview flowchart that Jean planned to give students instruction on five main points, represented by rectangles labeled "instruction."

the purpose of freewriting

timed freewriting

untimed freewriting

focused freewriting

keeping a journal

The lesson-overview flowchart also indicates that, for at least four of these points (timed freewriting, untimed freewriting, focused freewriting, and keeping a journal), Jean planned to have students engage in on-screen writing exercises that will be evaluated in some way. She designated the exercises with rectangles labeled "exercises," and she marked the evaluation of these exercises with diamonds labeled "test." Tests involve a decision about students' performances on an activity. As Jean indicated with her arrows, an unacceptable answer on these tests would require students to recycle back through more instruction on the same point and another exercise. An acceptable answer would allow them to go on to the next instructional point.

At this time, you need to think about how you'd represent your own CAI project in a lesson-overview flowchart. At the end of this chapter, on Worksheet 9: Making a Lesson-Overview Flowchart, you will be asked to draw the first draft of such a diagram. Before you begin the work of creating the lesson-overview flowchart, however, it would make sense to review your task-analysis list, making sure that you have represented each activity and concept to be covered within the CAI lesson you are planning.

Example of Making a Lesson-Overview Flow Chart

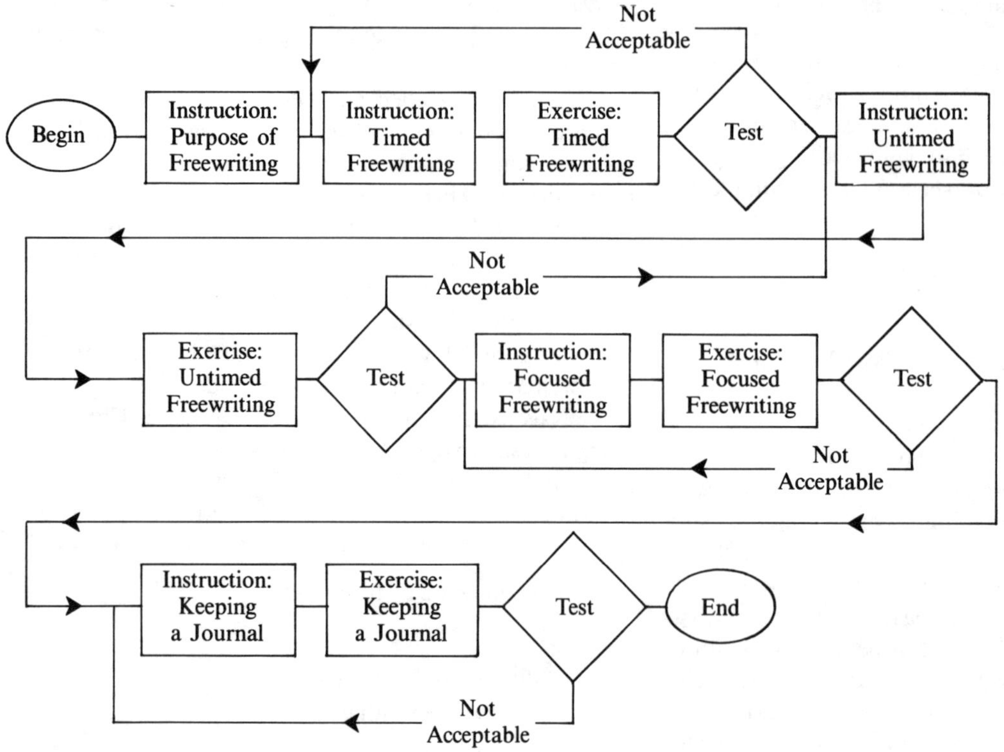

Figure 2.2: Sample of Worksheet 9 Activity

You might also want to review the organization of these tasks. Are they in an order that accurately reflects a realistic teaching sequence? If not, what order might be more appropriate? When you have reviewed your task-analysis list for accuracy, you can then use it to draw a lesson-overview flowchart. It may take several revisions of this diagram to get the elements of your chart just as you want them, but the finished flowchart will provide you with a basis for making many decisions about your CAI lesson later in the writing process.

If you want to try your hand at creating a lesson-overview flowchart, you may turn to Worksheet 9 and begin the process of assembling such a diagram. Some readers may prefer to finish reading the rest of this chapter first.

7. Beginning a Script of a CAI Lesson

The last predesign task we have identified for the composition specialist may be the easiest because it involves writing not lists or flowcharts, but good old-fashioned prose scripts, a task with which we are all familiar.

At the most basic level, writing CAI is no different from writing a script of a lesson—a written record that tells what the lesson should include, how the lesson should proceed, and what student responses will be acceptable at various points in the lesson.

Writing the first draft of this script, especially if you want the computer to mirror your own teaching style, is mostly a matter of writing down what you would say or do in the more comfortable setting of your own classroom. However, following a few basic guidelines as you start drafting can help ensure the value of a script in later stages of the composing process. These brief guidelines are explained in the following items and illustrated in a sample script in figures 2.3 and 2.4.

1. Print the script on copies of Worksheet 10.[1] Only print between one and twenty-two lines per sheet. Think of these sheets as screens on the computer. One sheet will contain as much information as (and look just like) one screen in the final CAI lesson. Each line of the sheet should contain no more than sixty characters. This will ensure ten character margins on each side of a standard eighty-character screen.

Example of Scripting a CAI Lesson

Screen Description: __Purpose of Freewriting__

Column

```
         1         10        20        30        40        50        60
         1234567890123456789012345678901234567890123456789012345678901234567890
Line  1  Many experts feel that freewriting can help you crystallize
      2  the vague shadow-like thoughts that linger at the back of
      3  your mind. In fact, some people suggest that writing,
      4  because it involves translating concepts into a symbolic
      5  system, necessarily involves both thinking and learning.
      6
      7  In the lesson that follows, we'll try to determine if this
      8  is true.
      9
     10
     11
     12
     13
     14
     15
     16
     17
     18
     19
     20  <G>o on, <B>ack up, <H>elp, <S>ave and <P>rint, <Q>uit
     21
     22
```

Notes:

Figure 2.3: Sample of Worksheet 10 Activity

Example of Scripting a CAI Lesson

Screen Description: Untimed Freewriting, Exercise, p. 3

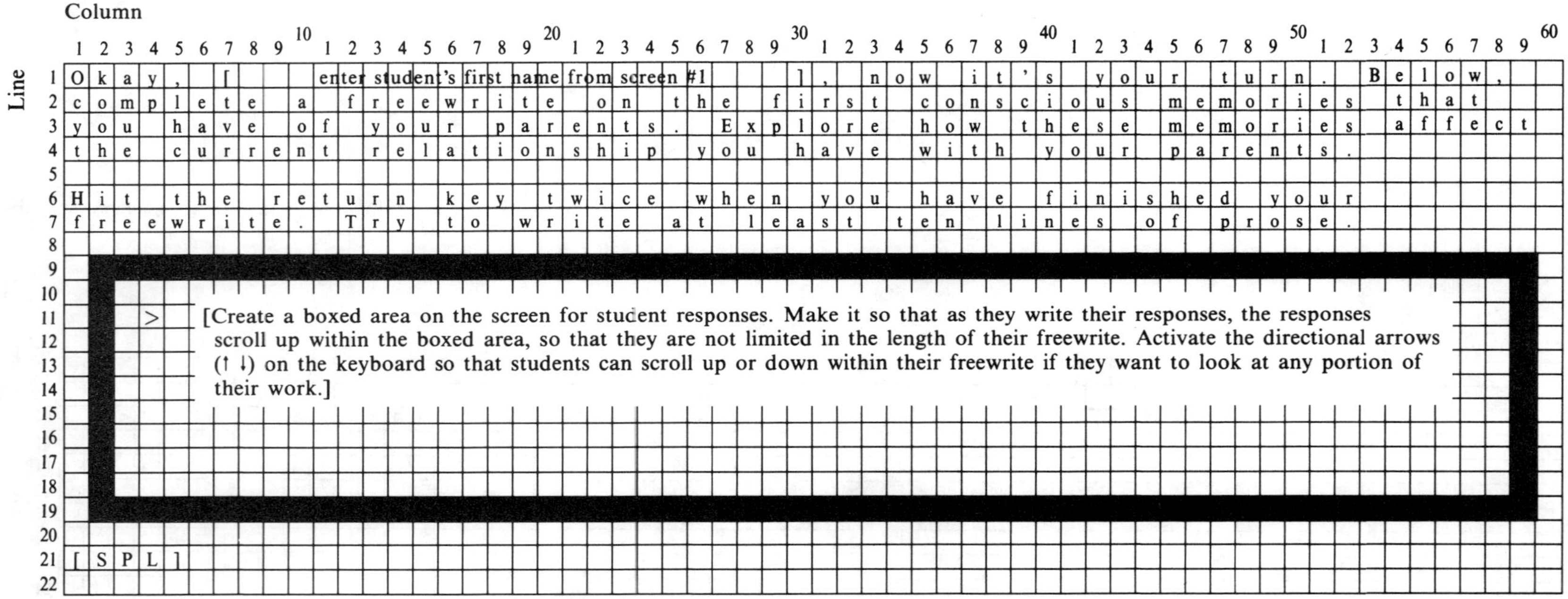

Column

```
            1         2         3         4         5         6
  12345678901234567890123456789012345678901234567890123456789012345678 90
1 Okay, [enter student's first name from screen #1], now it's your turn. Below,
2 complete a freewrite on the first conscious memories that
3 you have of your parents. Explore how these memories affect
4 the current relationship you have with your parents.
5
6 Hit the return key twice when you have finished your
7 freewrite. Try to write at least ten lines of prose.
8
9
10
11 >
```

[Create a boxed area on the screen for student responses. Make it so that as they write their responses, the responses scroll up within the boxed area, so that they are not limited in the length of their freewrite. Activate the directional arrows (↑↓) on the keyboard so that students can scroll up or down within their freewrite if they want to look at any portion of their work.]

```
21 [ S P L ]
```

Notes: [Branching instructions: If response in box is less than ten lines, go to
Untimed Freewrite, Test p. 1. If response is ten lines or more, go to
Untimed Freewrite, Test p. 2.]

Figure 2.4: Sample of Worksheet 10 Activity

2. On each script worksheet, write exactly what you want the computer to print on the screen.

3. You will probably want to identify a standard line of choices that will appear at the bottom of most screens in your CAI lesson. We will refer to this as a *standard choice line.* Among your standard choices, think about including such commands as ⟨G⟩o forward one screen, ⟨B⟩ack up one screen, ⟨Q⟩uit this lesson, ⟨H⟩elp, ⟨S⟩ave and print this response, etc. Some screens in your lesson, depending on their purpose, may require a nonstandard choice line. (See Chapter Six: Thinking about Screen Display for more information about screen design.)

4. Don't worry about printing out the standard choice line at the bottom of every sheet; put the initials SCL (Standard Choice Line) instead.

5. In the upper left-hand corner of each screen worksheet, indicate the task that the screen is designed to help you teach. Jean's example shows a screen that is part of a task labeled "untimed freewriting." The screen is part of a practice exercise that Jean might want students to try after they learn some basics about what untimed freewriting is.

6. For each lesson screen that requires a student response, use the section labeled "Programmer's Notes" at the bottom of the sheet. In this section, describe the criteria you want to establish for testing the students' input, for deciding which answers are acceptable and which are not. These criteria will determine which way the program will branch for individual students. Chapter Five: Integrating Response and Evaluation into a CAI Lesson will provide further information on how to handle the evaluation of students' responses in a CAI lesson.

7. Use brackets to indicate material that the computer programmer should retrieve from earlier student responses. Indicate not only what information the programmer should supply, but also where (on what sheet or screen) he or she can find the original response. Using this system, for example, you can ask students to type a list of possible writing topics on an early screen and then have the CAI lesson call up these topics and refer specifically to them on later screens.

8. Also use brackets to make notes about special instructions for your programmer. If, for ex-

ample, you want students to enter their responses in a certain area of the screen or to limit their responses to a certain number of words, note it in brackets to inform your programmer.

9. Be sure to include clear and complete directions for the student and for the programmer. If, for example, you ask the students to do some writing on the screen, give them some method of indicating to the programmer when they are done with their entry.

Now that you know what scripts look like, you can begin to create some screens of your own for the CAI lesson you have planned. In fact, at the end of this chapter, we have provided Worksheet 10: Scripting a CAI Lesson, for this purpose. Don't worry if it takes you quite a while to get the hang of scripting on the grid we have provided; it may seem awkward and restrictive at first, but it will save you and your programmer a great deal of time and a great many headaches later in the process of developing your CAI lesson.[2]

Notes of Caution

Before you spend too much time scripting, you will want to read Chapters Four, Five, and Six in this book. These chapters provide you with additional information and advice about designing CAI that will have an impact on the scripts you produce. We suggest reading these chapters to get an overview of this advice *before* you try to create an entire script of your lesson. In light of the information contained in these chapters, you might also want to revise some parts of your CAI lesson as you have planned it in previous chapters.

About Using This Book

A caution about process seems warranted at this point. We have, in this book, broken down the process of writing a CAI lesson into a series of easy-to-follow steps. The actual process of writing CAI, however, is never so neat or clean-cut.

Like any process, writing CAI is both recursive and complex. You may, for example, get as far as creating a flowchart before you decide to go back and do some more brainstorming about a completely different topic. Or you may choose to spend days brainstorming and exploring several different topic choices before you begin to focus your instruction.

Don't worry, and don't let the steps we've outlined here limit or hinder your own natural problem-solving processes.

We are convinced, in fact, that revision should mark efforts *throughout* the design process. Don't be surprised if, as you work through the steps outlined in this book, you keep going back to the worksheets you have already completed and making changes in the shape, the content, or the scope of the lesson you are planning. The process of creating successful CAI lessons, like all other writing processes, involves rough starts, dead ends, multiple drafts, and rethinkings of the original concept. It would be a serious underestimation of the task to think that any author could take a straight-line, linear approach to creating sophisticated, successful CAI lessons.

Finally, the guidelines we have presented suggest only one way of approaching the design of a CAI lesson.[3] Use what you can, when you can. Adapt our steps to your writing process and never hesitate to go back, rewrite, revise, and rework your initial ideas.

Summary

In this chapter we have suggested seven predesign tasks that should be completed before work on a CAI lesson is begun. We believe that these preliminary steps will eliminate a great deal of authors' frustration once they begin writing a lesson and also help them avoid disappointment once the lesson is ready for use in an actual composition program. Successful CAI lessons result when authors are deliberate in making sure that their instructional material is informed by their rhetorical and pedagogical assumptions, that it is created carefully and with an eye toward use in a real classroom.

Notes

1. The screen-by-screen worksheets provided in this chapter are only models. Your computer screen may allow the use of more characters in each line or more lines on each screen. We encourage you to adapt these worksheets to fit the particular computer on which you will be working. Consult your programmer if you are not sure of screen dimensions.

2. The process of screen-by-screen scripting we have outlined here is certainly not the only such system that exists. Some authors prefer to use a sheet of large-grid graph paper to represent each computer screen. Other authors use a word-processing or graphics program to produce screen templates and the text that will appear on these screens. We are sure there are many other such systems. In any case, choose the system with which you are most comfortable, and be sure you know the exact screen dimensions (characters per line and lines per screen) with which you must work before you begin scripting.

3. Some authors, for example, would say that the process described in this book is needlessly complex and laborious when compared to the process of creating a lesson using a computerized authoring system (CDS-1, BLOCKS 82, and CAIWARE-2D are just a few such systems). Authoring systems are designed to facilitate the development of CAI exercises. A teacher will sit down at a computer, put in an authoring-system program, and then answer—using the keyboard—a series of questions that appear on the computer screen: What is the name of the exercise? How many items does the teacher want to cover on this exercise? How are they to be sequenced? What items should appear on the test? Which answers should be counted as correct? How many times are students allowed to try any given exercise? When the questions have been answered, the authoring system will produce the exercises as they have been defined by the teacher.

Unfortunately, none of the authoring systems we have seen (of those that were commercially available at the time of this printing) were designed with composition teachers or writing instruction in mind. Authoring systems we have used, for example, often presuppose an objective-question format, which limits the length of answers a student may type in, or an objective-testing format, which assumes a "right" or "wrong" answer for each response a student types in. Such frameworks are obviously inappropriate for most writing instruction. We remain convinced that current systems are extremely limited in their vision of the kind of teaching that goes on in a composition classroom or a writing lab, that they seldom allow teachers (even those who are willing) to produce lessons that reflect the theory and research now accepted in the field of writing.

We believe the low-tech, screen-by-screen system outlined in this book allows for a much more open-ended process of lesson design than do the authoring systems we've used, and, furthermore, that it can result in lessons that are as sound, theoretically and pedagogically, as more conventional instruction.

We understand that efforts are now underway at the University of Minnesota to construct an authoring system that will accommodate the teaching approaches of composition instructors. The project is headed by Lillian Bridwell and Donald Ross.

Worksheet 4: Ranking Student Writing Problems

In the space provided below, rank the clusters of student writing problems you identified on Worksheet 1: Identifying Student Writing Problems and give a few examples of the problems that typify each cluster.

Rank _____   Rank _____

Cluster _____   Cluster _____

Rank _____   Rank _____

Cluster _____   Cluster _____

Worksheet 5: Adjusting the Focus of a CAI Lesson

Larger Lesson   Medium-Sized Lesson   Smaller Lesson

Title: Title: Title:

Content: Content: Content:

Worksheet 6: Completing a Task Analysis of a CAI Lesson

In the space provided below, identify the topic around which you would like to organize your CAI lesson. Next, list the concepts that are crucial to an understanding of this topic and the activities you would employ in your classroom to teach this topic. At the bottom of the page, make any notations you may think of for adapting the topic, or the tasks you have identified, to the medium of computer-assisted instruction.

Topic:

Subtopics:

Notes:

Worksheet 7: Determining the Context for a CAI Lesson

Use your answers from Worksheet 2: Identifying Assumptions about Writing, your answers from Worksheet 3: Identifying Assumptions about Teaching Writing, and your evolving ideas about the CAI lesson you want to write to answer the following questions:

Purpose of Lesson

CAI Lesson and Assumptions about Writing

1.

Comments:

2.

Comments:

3.

Comments:

4.

Comments:

CAI Lesson and Assumptions about Teaching Writing

1.

Comments:

2.

Comments:

3.

Comments:

4.

Comments:

Worksheet 7 continued

Worksheet 8: Fitting CAI into the Writing Classroom/Program

Use your own experience in the classroom and your evolving ideas about your CAI lesson to answer the following questions:

1. When will students use the CAI lesson? At what point during my instructional sequence do I expect them to use the lesson?

2. Where will my students use the CAI lesson?

3. How long will students need to spend on the CAI lesson? Will this time be a supplement to or a substitute for regular classroom instruction?

4. Does the CAI lesson need to be documented or explained before the students use it? Are any supplemental reading or writing materials needed?

Worksheet 9: Making a Lesson-Overview Flow Chart

Using the three types of symbols we discussed earlier in this chapter—*ovals,* for beginnings and endings; *rectangles,* for "instruction" and "exercise" segments; and *diamonds,* for "test" activities—create a lesson-overview flow chart of your CAI lesson.

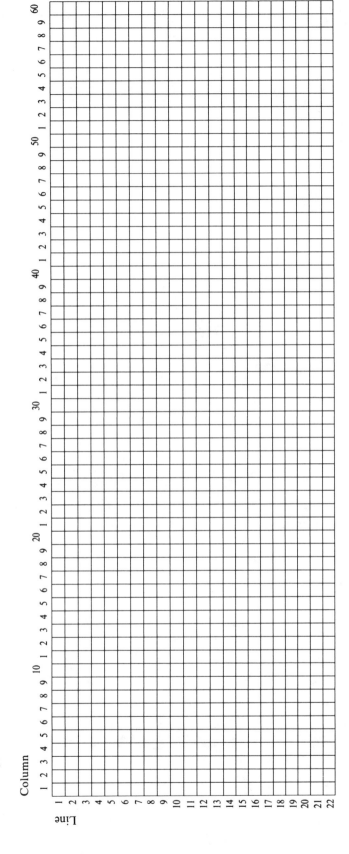

Worksheet 10: Scripting a CAI Lesson

Use copies of this grid to determine what part of your lesson will appear on each screen.

Screen Description: _____

Column

Line

Notes:

3 WORKING WITH A DESIGN TEAM

In previous chapters, we described the tasks of choosing a topic to address in a CAI lesson, deciding how the lesson would fit into an existing writing program or classroom, and scripting an initial draft of the lesson. But how, after starting on a CAI project, do authors proceed? How do they take the idea of a CAI project from its initial conception to the point where it can be used by students in a writing classroom or by other faculty in a writing program?

In most cases, the process of creating a polished CAI lesson requires the talents of more than one person. As English, rhetoric, or composition teachers, we are seldom trained to master the fields of software design, programming, statistics, or marketing. And yet, all these specialties may be required to produce a successful piece of CAI. To resolve this dilemma, we suggest forming a design team, a group of specialists with complementary talents who can work together to take an initial idea and turn it into a valuable CAI lesson for use in the composition classroom.

This chapter discusses how to form and work with a design team to create CAI lessons for writing-intensive classes. The following pages address three central questions connected with such a venture:

1. How does a design team work?
2. Who leads the design team?
3. Who should be included on the design team?

As you will see, the central theme of this chapter is that very few people have expertise in all the areas demanded by a complex CAI project and that even fewer have the time necessary to tackle such a project alone. Software design teams, modeled on similar groups that function in industry and business settings, represent collections of specialists with complementary skills. Such groups provide a range of expertise in the areas we have identified and make it possible to produce CAI lessons that are technically sophisticated, theoretically sound, and pedagogically effective.

How Does a Design Team Work?

The basic concept of a design team is far from new. Any group or committee that has pooled the talents and skills of individuals to accomplish a desired goal has experienced the advantages of such a team. In this text, the term "design team" will be used to refer to a specially formulated group of experts who cooperate to create CAI lessons or software for writing-intensive classes or programs.

Although design teams of the kind that we describe share a common goal (that of producing CAI for the composition classroom), they differ widely in their constitution. Generally speaking, the design teams we are describing are formed and led by composition specialists who have a personal stake in creating CAI lessons for composition-intensive classes. As a result, the membership of a design team will depend on the personality of this team leader and the requirements of the CAI project under consideration.

An economical team, for example, may consist of a simple collaborative effort on the part of two colleagues with complementary skills. Other design teams will have more elaborate memberships and will involve students as well as teachers. The team we will use for discussion purposes throughout this book consists of four members: a composition specialist, a programmer, an educational specialist, and a marketing specialist. We should add, however, that any number of other experts could be valuable contributors to a team effort. Depending on the CAI project being planned, the team might want to involve linguists, reading specialists, cognitive psychologists, literature teachers, or other experts.

Because design teams are shaped by the academic institutions within which they function, their internal structure, methods of operation, and support they enjoy will also vary widely. Some teams, for instance, meet regularly, much like a committee, to consider the progress being made on a CAI project. Other teams are less formal, communicating via telephone conversations or in casual hallway meetings. In addition, depending on the personality of the composition specialists who head the team, some groups tend to be leader-oriented and others to be marked by a loosely democratic structure. Finally, some design teams are fortunate enough to have access to institutional financial resources that buy released time for their members during the summer or even the academic year. Other teams must rely on all-volunteer efforts from their members.

In short, there are no rules governing the formation and operation of a software-design team. These groups succeed best when they are responsive to the setting in which they are formed, the motivation of their members and leaders, and the nature of the CAI project they will tackle.

Who Should Lead the Design Team?

Perhaps the most important member of the design team, at least as that group will be represented in this book, is the composition specialist. As the primary author of the CAI lesson, the composition specialist acts as team leader, content specialist, and curriculum expert. We do not make this claim lightly, nor as a manifestation of chauvinistic pride in our profession. A basic premise of this book is that the best and most effective CAI lessons for use in composition classrooms grow organically from the needs and the philosophy of a specific writing class or writing program. The catalyst for this process, and indeed the focus of the team effort, must be the teacher of composition.

The composition specialist's role, however, may change with the progress of the project as indicated in figure 3.1.

Early in the project, the composition specialist, as the primary author, may take a central role in the software-design effort: making initial philosophical decisions about the value and the place of CAI in a composition program or classroom, the pedagogical and rhetorical assumptions upon which CAI should be based, and the possible content of individual CAI lessons. In addition, the composition specialist will probably have to assume the burden of getting the project off the ground, lining up funding for the effort, identifying the other members of the design team, and consulting with these individuals.

As the project progresses, after the composition specialist has focused the concept and content of the lesson, created a satisfactory overview of the instruc-

tion, and drafted a successful screen-by-screen script of the lesson as it will appear on the computer monitor, he or she may find it easier to rely on other members of the design team. The programmer, for example, may start to become more prominent in the design process, translating the author's instructional material into a code that the computer can under-

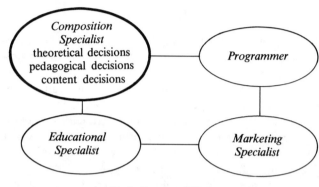

Early Stages of Project

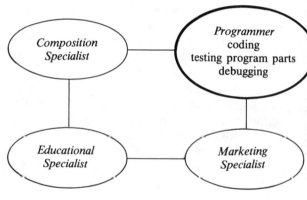

Middle Stages of Project

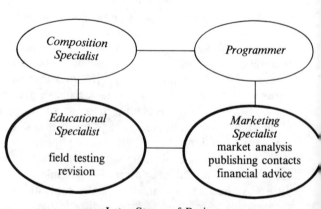

Later Stages of Project

Figure 3.1: Design Team Roles

stand. At this point, the composition specialist may still serve as an active consultant, advising the programmer on specific program requirements.

At the later stages of the project, when the initial round of coding (programming) is done, the composition specialist and the programmer may fade into the background for a short period, while a different team member, such as the educational consultant, takes over the field testing of the lesson and suggests revisions based on this field testing. Other team members, such as the marketing specialist, for instance, may also assume a more active role in the later stages of the design process, especially if the team plans to disseminate the CAI lesson to a wider audience.

At every stage of the project, however, the composition specialist, as team leader, will want to monitor the decisions being made with regard to the CAI lesson to ensure that it remains faithful to the original intention of the instruction and to the premises that underlie the writing classroom or program in which it will be used. For example, it is the composition specialist who will need to explain the theory and the philosophy behind the writing activity when a programmer suggests that multiple choice answers would be better for the lesson than essay answers because they are "easier to program."

Similarly, it is the composition specialist who will want to assume the responsibility for monitoring the pedagogical integrity of the lesson as a piece of writing instruction. It will be up to the composition specialist, for instance, to answer team members who suggest that every one of the students' written responses in a CAI lesson should be evaluated as correct or incorrect. In such cases, by drawing on experience in writing-intensive classes as well as recent research and theory in the field of writing, the composition specialist can illustrate how writing involves learning and thinking regardless of whether or not activities are assessed formally.

Who Should Be Included on the Design Team?

As we noted earlier, any number of specialists can contribute to the success of a design team. As the team leader, however, the composition specialist will probably assume the primary role in determining a team's membership. Membership decisions will also be a function of the CAI project itself; different lessons require the talents of different specialists. A lesson on syntax, for example, may require extensive consultation with a linguist; a lesson on the writing process may involve a cognitive psychologist as a member of the design team.

For the purposes of this discussion, however, we will leave the choice of content-area specialists up to you. As the plans for your CAI lessons become more firm, the decisions about content-area consultants will clarify themselves. What we can do in this section is suggest some guidelines for selecting three other experts commonly invited to join a software design team: a programmer, an educational specialist, and a marketing expert.

Choosing a Programmer

According to the team structure we describe in this book, a programmer translates the author's written scripts into a code using some computer language (BASIC, COBOL, Pascal, C) or an authoring language (a specialized computer language that allows programmers to use abbreviated commands to accomplish complex tasks more efficiently). Optimally, the team's programmer should be proficient in a number of computer languages. With this skill, the programmer can choose a language that runs on the computers in any given educational setting or on certain popular brands of computers that are found in a number of different settings. Knowledge of a "transportable" programming language can be especially important if the team plans to market the CAI lesson for use by other teachers.

In addition, the programmer should be interested in and enthusiastic about the team's CAI project. A programmer who is disinterested or even antipathetic toward writing and writing instruction may turn out to be a drain on the group's time and energy. A programmer who writes frequently or who struggles with writing problems may be able to provide some new perspectives on the very topic the team is treating in the CAI lesson.

Perhaps the *most* important qualification for a team programmer is that he or she be able to communicate clearly in terms that all group members can understand. For this reason, we suggest interviewing a number of prospective programmers and choosing the best possible applicant for the design team. If, in interviewing a programmer, you find yourself feeling left out, stupid, or inadequate—go no further. You need a programmer who can explain very technical matters in plain language, one who can document programs in clear English. If the programmer cannot communicate during a short interview, it is likely that he or she will be of little help in thrashing out complex problems in a meeting of the design team.

As the composition specialist and the primary author on your design team, beware of programmers who tell you that things can't be done or that there is only one way of translating the group's ideas into code. The job of a programmer is to choose a language and coding algorithms that *will* do what you want. A good programmer will not begin an interview by asking you to change the CAI lesson you have planned to accommodate a favorite programming language or a personal conception of the way computer-assisted instruction should look.

If you are less than confident in dealing with programmers and these feelings keep you from being effective in communicating as you interview programmers for your design team, try auditing a beginning programming class at your local community college, adult school, or university. Such a course, even if you don't complete it, will help demystify computers for you and provide explanations of the logical processes in which computers can engage. It will also allow you to acquire a vocabulary that you can use to trade ideas with the programming member of the design team.

Where do you find a programmer? Perhaps the best place to look is right in your own college, high school, or classroom. Often college students majoring in computer science are excellent candidates. Quite frequently, these students must complete an independent, large-scale programming project as part of their degree. In any case, they are eager to undertake a coding project for a minimal hourly fee. One hint may be useful, if you are looking for college students to act as members of your design team: look for sophomores or juniors who have completed their study of several programming languages, but who also have one or two years of study left before they move on. These individuals prove to be especially helpful if the CAI project you have in mind will extend over a longer period of time.

Increasingly, high school students are also becoming skilled enough to undertake a large programming task. With these students, look for maturity as well as knowledge of several programming languages. You will be communicating with these people about very sophisticated concepts and tasks, and they must have the intellectual maturity to understand you.

Of course, students are not the only answer to your programming needs. Often, colleagues express interest in projects that involve collaboration across normal curricular boundaries. You might try trading your services as coauthor, editor, or proofreader with a colleague in computer science for the time he or she spends on your CAI lesson. The same approach can be used with professional programmers who work in industrial settings. Although these people may charge more than you could afford if you were to hire them, they may be persuaded to trade their services for your expertise on a project they want to undertake. In all cases, make sure that the programmer you choose has some interest in your project, either because this person is a writer or because he or she believes in the importance of the instructional goals you are trying to achieve with your CAI lesson.

A final suggestion for choosing a programmer involves keeping track of the individuals you consider for this position. Be systematic about recording information as you interview programming candidates so that you can eventually make an informed decision about the person you ask to join the team. Keeping thorough records of the programmers you interview will also allow you to replace, as expeditiously as possible, programmers who, for one reason or another, might have to leave the design team in the middle of your project. Constructing and filling out a standard interview form for each programming applicant will assist you in this effort. In figure 3.2, you see one example of such a form as it might have been completed by Jean when she formed her software-design team.

At the end of this chapter, we have provided you with an interview form, Worksheet 11: Choosing a Programmer, that you can use to gauge the suitability of the programmers with which you talk. It should also provide you with a record of the information you obtain in interviewing situations.

Choosing an Educational Specialist

Choosing an educational specialist to serve on the design team may not involve the same problems as choosing a programmer, but such a specialist can, nonetheless, be an important member of the group. The educational specialist can provide advice on the range of cognitive skills the CAI lesson is addressing (e.g., Is the lesson engaging students in higher level skills like synthesizing and analyzing information rather than just asking them to memorize information?), the presentation of the information (e.g., Are students asked to respond actively to instruction on almost every screen?), and the field testing and evaluation of the lesson itself.

Example of Choosing a Programmer

Name: Doria McNulty

Address: 1629 Austin St., Columbia, MO 49931

Telephone: 443-4983

Programming Languages: (circle)

PASCAL   COBOL   C

BASIC   SNOBOL   Others: LISP

Authoring Systems/Languages: CDS 1, COMMON PILOT, TUTOR

Ability to Communicate/Explain Ideas in Plain Language:

excellent   medium   poor

Willingness to Find a Way to Do What I Want Done:

excellent   medium   poor

Interest in Project:

excellent   medium   poor

Comments: McNulty has an undergraduate degree in Liberal Arts and says that she enjoyed her writing classes in college. She also emphasized her strengths in writing documentation for her programs. She exhibited enthusiasm about the Freewrite design project and hinted that she may be willing to exchange programming time for editing help on several professional articles she is trying to write.

Figure 3.2: Sample of Worksheet 11 Activity

Again, as primary author and team leader, you may want to interview several educational specialists before deciding which one would be the most amenable to your ideas about CAI. In choosing an educational specialist, look for someone who has had experience with computerized instruction. Such a person can suggest motivational devices that might be added to your program (graphics, timed exercises, scoring competitions, games, rewards), ways to individualize the instruction that the lesson offers (menus, answer-dependent branching, retrieval of previous responses), and creative methods of assessing the appropriateness of a student's written responses (searching for key words or phrases, providing self-evaluation guidelines, providing matching samples).

The educational specialist can also supervise the field testing and evaluation of the lesson at various stages of completion if he or she has had some experience in evaluating educational materials and their effectiveness. In the later stages of the project, the educational specialist should be able to construct a systematic plan for testing each important element of the CAI lesson to measure its impact on student learning. This kind of modularized testing can provide specific suggestions for revising the weaker or less effective parts of the CAI lesson. In Chapter Seven: Field Testing CAI Lessons, we have made some additional suggestions about field testing that you may want to go over with the team's educational specialist during the later stages of the CAI project.

Settling on remuneration for an educational specialist's time may exercise your creativity. Some authors suggest thinking in terms of alternatives to traditional educational funding sources: trade professional services (editing, proofreading, coauthoring) for consulting time, pay a nominal fee, or offer part of the profits from the lesson if it is to be marketed for a larger audience.

Although educational specialists with the ideal qualifications outlined above may be harder to find than programmers, we still suggest that you be systematic about recording impressions of the people you approach. You might only interview two or three educational specialists for your design team, but it never hurts to keep track of individuals' qualifications. You may find, later in the design process, that such information comes in handy. For example, keeping careful notes on an educational specialist who mentions contacts in the state educational agency during an interview may allow you to remind the team of possible field-testing populations or marketing spheres near

the end of a project. In figure 3.3, you will see one sample of an interview form for educational specialists as Jean might have completed it.

At the end of this chapter, we have provided a similar form, Worksheet 12: Choosing an Educational Specialist, to help you keep track of the educational specialists you interview.

Choosing a Marketing Specialist

If, as the primary author of a CAI lesson, you are planning to disseminate this product to a larger audience than those teachers within your department, you may want to ask a marketing or business specialist to join the design team. A good business consultant can plan an initial marketing strategy for the CAI package, write product descriptions and hardware specifications, contact publishers and software distributors, and conduct final product negotiations.

As the composition expert on your team, you will need to work closely with any business consultant. He or she will have to know, for example, whom you see as the target audiences for the lesson (remember, although students will use the lesson, teachers, principals, and lab directors may be the people who buy it), what the members of this audience value in a CAI lesson (teachers may value instructional content primarily, while principals are looking for reasonable prices, and students for motivating instruction), and finally, what the customers need in terms of product support (documentation, accompanying handbooks, follow-up technical services).

Again, you will have to negotiate with marketing specialists about the return they expect for investing their time in your project. If you are convinced that your project will sell well in the open market, you might be able to promise a portion of the eventual profits. You might also be in a position to trade professional services (editing, proofreading, ghostwriting) for consulting expertise in the field of marketing.

Finally, we suggest filling out a short interview sheet on each marketing specialist you interview for the design team. These sheets will provide pertinent data on each candidate and can help you compare the qualifications of the various individuals before you make a final selection. In figure 3.4, you can see a sample form for interviewing marketing specialists that Jean might have completed during the process of putting together her own design team.

At the end of this chapter, we will provide you with a similar form, Worksheet 13: Choosing a

Example of Choosing an Educational Specialist

Name: ___Dan Beemer___

Address: ___202 S. 4th St., Columbia, MO 49931___

Telephone: ___443-5963___

Areas of Specialization:

CAI: Beemer is just out of college, but he did take several courses on educational uses of CAI while he was at the State U. He seems eager to try a full-scale project.

Evaluation/Testing: Reports taking two courses on educational testing and evaluation—one under Dr. E. Kelter. He suggested several books that might be good background reading for the team:

Godfrey & Sterling, *The Elements of CAI* Burke, *CAI Sourcebook*

Field Testing: Has never really tested any CAI although he says he is familiar with several different systems for observing students as they use CAI and recording their reactions. Has had experience with protocol analysis.

Writing: Is certainly positive about writing. Says he is writing his own science fiction novel.

Ability to Communicate/Explain Ideas:

excellent   (medium)   poor

Willingness to Find a Way to Do What I Want Done:

(excellent)   medium   poor

Interest in Project:

(excellent)   medium   poor

Comments: Beemer is young but extremely enthusiastic about the Freewriting project. I like his frankness and his ideas about testing methodology.

Figure 3.3: Sample of Worksheet 12 Activity

Example of Choosing a Marketing Specialist

Name: _____Sandra Kelley_____

Address: __2243 Cobalt Ave., Columbia, MO 49931_____

Telephone: __442-8853_____

Areas of Specialization:

CAI: Kelley teaches in the Business Department. She is thinking about trying to set up her own software marketing operation on the side. She has worked with computers in her own field and has used quite a few CAI programs designed for business and industry.

Publishing Contacts: She reviews business software programs for several small publishers: LIVEWARE and NEWSOFT. Says she knows the editors there.

Marketing Software: Only her reviewing experience. Hasn't really marketed any software yet. Seems familiar enough with marketing principles in general though.

Writing: Hated English in college, but doesn't seem to mind writing for professional reasons. She did say that she thought writing was important for people in her field.

Ability to Communicate/Explain Ideas:

excellent   (medium)   poor

Willingness to Find a Way to Do What I Want Done:

(excellent)   medium   poor

Interest in Project:

excellent   (medium)   poor

Comments: Very quiet, but seemed determined about starting her own business. When she talked about marketing, enthusiasm increased.

Figure 3.4: Sample of Worksheet 13 Activity

Marketing Specialist, to help you keep track of the marketing specialists you interview for the design team. You may want to turn to that section now and look over this worksheet.

Summary

In this chapter, we have discussed how design teams work; talked about the role of the composition specialist in leading such a team; explored the formation of a typical design team consisting of a composition specialist, a programmer, an educational specialist, and a marketing specialist; and discussed the contributions each of these members can make to a CAI design project.

Ultimately, however, the choice of team members rests with you, as the team leader and primary author, and will be determined by your own unique situation. Thus, the suggestions we have provided will be useful only if they are modified to fit a specific project. Some authors may find, for example, that they can function perfectly well with only a two-person team consisting of a composition specialist and a programmer. In such cases, the rather formal processes we have suggested for interviewing and record keeping may prove unnecessary. In other cases, authors may choose to combine the expertise of three or four composition specialists, a cluster of programmers, an educational specialist, and a marketing specialist. For these situations, the process we have outlined may seem more valuable. In any case, we encourage you to experiment with the talent you have available to create a design team that will function effectively. Do not let our suggestions constrain either the size or the makeup of the team that you gather together.

As team leader, you will also be responsible for funding the team's efforts, and this might well prove to be the hardest part of your job. Although you can donate your own time to the project, it may be hard to convince other team members to do the same. In the previous sections, we suggested some alternatives to traditional sources of educational funding, but we encourage you not to let these ideas limit your thinking about funding. Continue to explore public- and private-sector grants, research and curriculum-development awards from local and national professional organizations, and scholarships.

In addition, do not overlook those sources in your own backyard; most educational institutions have some source of funds for innovative pedagogical projects. If you can convince administrators that your CAI lesson will make a significant contribution to communication curricula or to the education of students in general, you might have a good shot at such monies. Although these discretionary awards are becoming scarce as school budgets are tightened, the increased emphasis on computer-assisted education may, in itself, lend weight to your arguments.

One final note, every design team differs slightly in makeup, membership, and function. As a result, and in an effort to talk directly to an audience of our colleagues, we have structured the remaining chapters of this book so that they explore the team-design process from the perspective of the composition specialist. As team leader, you will have to translate and then apply the advice you find within these pages to your own team situation.

Worksheet 11: Choosing a Programmer

Name: _____

Address: _____

Telephone: _____

Programming Languages: (circle)

        PASCAL   COBOL   C

        BASIC   SNOBOL   Others: _____

Authoring Systems/Languages:

Ability to Communicate/Explain Ideas in Plain Language:

excellent   medium   poor

Willingness to Find a Way to Do What I Want Done:

excellent   medium   poor

Interest in Project:

excellent   medium   poor

Comments:

Worksheet 12: Choosing an Educational Specialist

Name: _____

Address: _____

Telephone: _____

Areas of Specialization:

      CAI:

      Evaluation/Testing:

      Field Testing:

      Writing:

Ability to Communicate/Explain Ideas:

excellent   medium   poor

Willingness to Find a Way to Do What I Want Done:

excellent   medium   poor

Interest in Project:

excellent   medium   poor

Comments:

Worksheet 13: Choosing a Marketing Specialist

Name: _____

Address: _____

Telephone: _____

Areas of Specialization:

    CAI:

    Publishing Contacts:

    Marketing Software:

    Writing:

Ability to Communicate/Explain Ideas:

cxccllcnt   medium   poor

Willingness to Find a Way to Do What I Want Done:

excellent   medium   poor

Interest in Project:

excellent   medium   poor

Comments:

4 MAKING PEDAGOGICAL DECISIONS ABOUT A CAI LESSON

The process we have outlined thus far involves choosing a topic for a CAI lesson, focusing the content and presentation of this lesson, and carefully analyzing the principles upon which the lesson will be based. In addition, we have discussed how to begin drafting a screen-by-screen script of the CAI lesson you want to create. Like all rough drafts, however, this initial script will probably undergo a number of major revisions before you are satisfied with it. In fact, writing CAI is like writing anything else; it is a process of refining and approximating, sometimes by very small steps. This chapter will discuss three important pedagogical considerations to keep in mind when you begin the task of revising a CAI lesson:

1. Define instructional objectives for the CAI lesson.

2. Identify possible screen types, or frame types, for use in the CAI lesson.

3. Think about concepts such as lesson design, lesson approach, and audience appropriateness in relation to the CAI lesson.

Defining Instructional Objectives

One of the first projects you will want to work on after writing a rough draft of a CAI lesson, is defining more precisely the instructional objectives for the instruction. Many teachers with whom we have worked cringe at the thought of writing instructional objectives. However, given the process we have outlined thus far in the book, this task should be a relatively painless one. You have already identified the general purpose of your CAI lesson and detailed those assumptions about teaching and writing that will inform this lesson. These predesign activities should facilitate your efforts to write instructional objectives for the lesson.

Instructional objectives, as we will talk about them in this book, are statements about the things authors want students to *know* or *do* after they complete a

CAI lesson. To write objectives, then, authors must define the specific goals they want to achieve with their instruction before it is ever written. For most teachers, this task takes quite a bit of thinking, and, at least in some ways, it seems to take some of the fun, the freshness, the improvisation out of teaching. Most of us modify our educational objectives as we teach, as we sense and respond to subtle clues about the mood, the interests, the momentum of our students on any given day. When we have to define the desired outcomes of a class artificially, before we ever meet with our students and size them up with a practiced eye, some of this spontaneity is lost.

And yet, especially with computer-assisted instruction, such careful anticipation and planning is necessary. We write CAI lessons, for the most part, so that we don't *have* to be there with our students at every step of the learning process. Instructional objectives force us to articulate more precisely vague learning goals so that we can trust computers to do some of the easier teaching tasks for us.

In the following example you'll see two objectives that Jean could have written for her CAI unit on freewriting. As you read these examples, note that each objective has three essential parts:

1. a *context* ("given . . ." and "using the . . ."),

2. an *action* ("list" and "write"), and

3. *testing criteria* for measurement ("at least fifteen possible freewriting topics" and "for at least ten minutes").

Example of Identifying Instructional Objectives

Subtopic: 2.0 Timed Freewriting

Objective: 2.1 Given instructional screens that explain what timed freewriting and brainstorming are and a short narrative writing assignment, students who use this CAI will be able to brainstorm a list of at least fifteen possible freewriting topics.

Objective: 2.2 Using the list of possible topics they have brainstormed, student users will be able to choose one topic and do a timed freewrite on it for at least ten minutes.

Jean's examples demonstrate several characteristics that would make a team's later design efforts easier:

1. She used a numbering system that identifies how each instructional objective is connected to those topics identified earlier in her task analysis (see page 17). The instructional objectives, identified here as Jean's, are numbered 2.1 and 2.2 because they correspond with the *second* topic on her task-analysis list: timed freewriting. Using this same system, she would number those instructional objectives associated with the *first* topic on her task analysis 1.1, 1.2, and so on. Objectives associated with the *third* topic on her task analysis would be numbered 3.1, 3.2, etc.

2. As measurement criteria, Jean's examples include things that the computer can do easily—counting fifteen brainstorming entries and keeping time for ten minutes. Although computers *cannot* read and understand prose, they *can* check students' responses in these other ways.

3. Jean's objectives were directly informed by the stated purpose of her CAI lesson and by the assumptions she identified about teaching and writing. Looking back at pages 17–18, for instance, you can see a direct link between Jean's theoretical and philosophical assumptions and the applications of these assumptions in the CAI lesson she is planning.

At the end of this chapter, you will be asked to write a series of instructional objectives for the CAI lesson your team is planning. This task will involve writing a great many objectives, each of which is associated with one of the topics included in the task analysis you did earlier (see Worksheet 6: Completing a Task Analysis of a CAI Lesson).

This activity, although time-consuming, is also beneficial; it requires you to make concrete your identification of the specific concepts and strategies you want to teach in connection with your CAI lesson. In fact, writing instructional objectives like the ones we have shown you here has several additional advantages.

1. Writing instructional objectives requires authors to identify a learning context within which students are expected to function. As a result,

careful plans must be made for moving students from step to step through the lesson. Although this regimented anticipation might seem artificial now, it will pay added dividends in well-thought-out CAI—especially if each objective is directly informed by previously stated assumptions about teaching and writing (see Worksheet 7: Determining the Context for a CAI Lesson).

2. Because all objectives stipulate some action that must be performed by students (e.g., "brainstorm a list," "choose a topic," or "do a timed freewrite"), they encourage active instructional experiences for students.

3. Because all instructional objectives include testing criteria for measuring successful completion, they serve as valuable methods of field testing and evaluating the effectiveness of a CAI lesson during later stages of the design process.

At the end of this chapter, we have provided Worksheet 14: Identifying Instructional Objectives on which you will be asked to write instructional objectives for the CAI lesson your team is planning. You can turn to that worksheet now or read the remainder of this chapter first to get an overview of the rest of the material it contains.

Whenever you begin the task of writing instructional objectives for your CAI lesson, you will want to go back and look at the topics and activities included in your original task analysis (i.e., Worksheet 6: Creating a Task Analysis of a CAI Lesson) and in your screen-by-screen lesson script. In this way, you can double-check your earlier work and make sure your plans for the CAI lesson are complete. You may find that the process of writing instructional objectives suggests new activities or topics that you did not think of earlier. Feel free to add these items to your task-analysis list.

Identifying Possible Screen Types

When we explained how to write the first draft of a CAI script, we encouraged authors to write down exactly "what you would say or do in the more comfortable setting of your classroom" so that the CAI lesson would mirror that teacher's normal style of instruction. We hoped, in this way, to avoid limiting authors' imagination by suggesting that only certain kinds of *screens* or *frames* (the amount of material that appears on a computer screen at any one time) could be used in a CAI lesson.

At this point in the process, however, you may be interested in seeing the variety of screen types that other CAI writers use. Unless you have seen quite a few different CAI programs in operation, it may be difficult to imagine the teaching techniques that can be used on a computer screen. In this section, we will survey a range of screen types to expand the repertoire from which you can draw in writing the next draft of your script. We will also ask you to identify where, in your script, you think some of these screen types might be useful.[1]

Introductory Screens

The very first screens that students see when they sit down to use your CAI will be the introductory screens. Figure 4.1 shows one example of an introductory screen. These screens may give the title of the CAI lesson, the title of the series in which the lesson is contained, the author's name and affiliation. In addition, introductory screens may provide copyright information; identify the grade level (or levels) for which the CAI is most appropriate; and provide information about the courseware's publication, distribution, or maintenance.

Because these screens introduce students to the CAI they are going to be using, it is important that they establish the tone that will be maintained throughout the lesson. In general, introductory screens are most effective when they are kept to a minimum; most users are quickly bored by these essentially passive frames. To reduce the number of introductory screens that must appear at the beginning of a lesson, some authors differentiate between *optional* and *mandatory* introductory information. Mandatory introductory screens appear for all lesson users every time they access the lesson. Optional introductory screens are kept hidden unless specifically requested by individual users. This optional arrangement makes for a more direct and efficient path through the CAI lesson and keeps students from being bored by unnecessary screens if they use the CAI lesson more than once or twice.

Orientation Screens

In longer lessons and in lessons that are part of a series, students may need additional information after the introductory screens to orient themselves. This is especially important because users cannot "see" all of a CAI lesson in one glance. Unlike a lesson in a book that students can leaf through quickly to see how far they have come and how far they have left to go, the bulk of a CAI lesson is hidden in a machine. This fact can be not only disconcerting to students but inconvenient if they have only limited amounts of time to work at the computer.

Orientation screens may locate the current lesson within a map of the entire series, provide information about how long the lesson takes to complete, give a brief prose statement about the purpose of the lesson or the series, or explain in general how the lesson is to proceed. The orientation screen in figure 4.2, for instance, helps student users gauge their progress within a long instructional sequence by highlighting their current position on a graphic lesson map.

Like mandatory introductory screens, mandatory orientation screens are best kept to a minimum. There is no reason, however, to limit the number of optional orientation screens that student users can access. The more such information you can make available to students, the less chance they have to become lost and frustrated when using your CAI lesson.

Help Screens

In lessons that contain complicated directions, it may be useful to provide screens that explain commands, menus, or keystrokes. Some series contain a sequence of help screens, also called "user's tutorials." Students can access these screens the first few times they use the material and can skip the material on subsequent exposures when they become more familiar with the common structure shared by the related lessons. Figure 4.3 illustrates a short help screen that explains the use of special function keys for a program called WordsWork.

In general, help screens, too, are most effective when they are optional rather than mandatory. The optional arrangement makes for a more direct path through the lesson and keeps students from being bombarded by unnecessary help information.

Menu Screens

In most lessons, teachers find it useful to provide students with choices of one sort or another. At some point in a CAI lesson, for example, a teacher may want students to choose between instruction on "timed" or "untimed" freewriting, or to decide whether they want to write sonnets, haiku, or blank verse. Menu screens allow instructors to present students

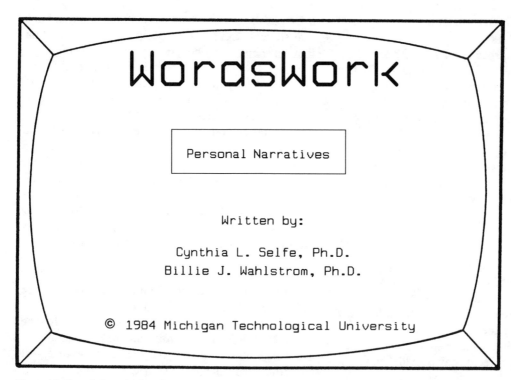

Figure 4.1: Sample Introduction Screen

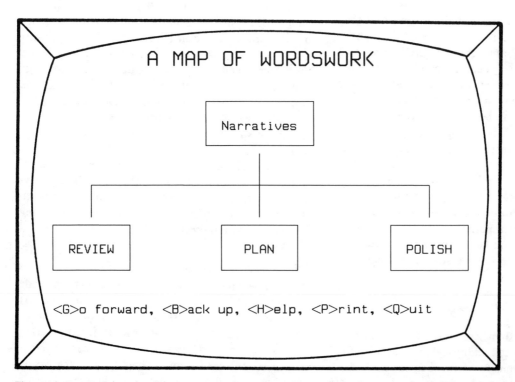

Figure 4.2: Sample Orientation Screen

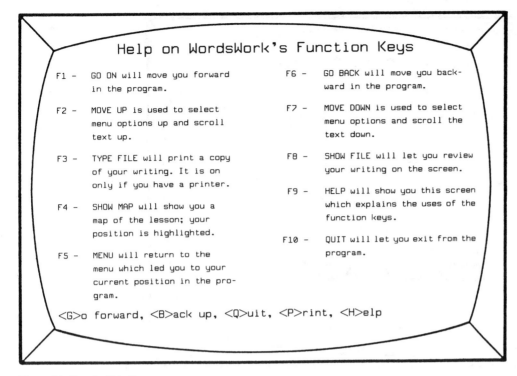

Figure 4.3: Sample Help Screen

with specific options from which to choose. Figure 4.4, for example, illustrates two different menu screens which ask students to choose the direction of their own instruction. On these screens, students make their choices by marking them with movable, highlighted boxes.

Menu screens, when they provide the opportunity for more than one choice of instructional sequence or direction, represent branches in a computer program. The more branches an author builds into a CAI lesson, the more individualized it will become for each student who uses it.

Instruction Screens

Perhaps the simplest screens authors write for a CAI lesson contain material they want the student to learn. These instruction screens, for example, might list for students the characteristics of memoranda, explain the differences between writing transactional and poetic discourse, illustrate the concept of paragraph cohesion, define subordination as it relates to style, or demonstrate the effect of word choice in a particular sentence. The screen in figure 4.5, for instance, instructs students by providing them with two example text passages to read and compare—one passage that illustrates "telling" and one that illustrates "showing."

Although a substantial percentage of screens in any CAI lesson will be instructional in nature, try not to use more than one or two in sequence. Instruction screens are presentational in nature, they are essentially *passive* rather than *active,* and can become boring when not interspersed with screens that demand user activity.

Exercise and Testing Screens

At various points in your CAI lesson, you will ask students to complete on-screen exercises that require a knowledge of the writing instruction that has been presented. We will call frames that ask for this kind of material "exercise screens." You might, for example, use an exercise screen to ask students to write a series of short character sketches, to summarize in a sentence or two their process of proofreading a paper, to list the characteristics of a good business letter, to compare the appeal of two prose passages, or to identify the focus of another student's paper. In figure 4.6, we provide a sample exercise screen that asks students to identify a character's motivation as illustrated in a short text passage.

CAI for writing classrooms can present special challenges for designing such screens because the responses that writing exercises require can be quite

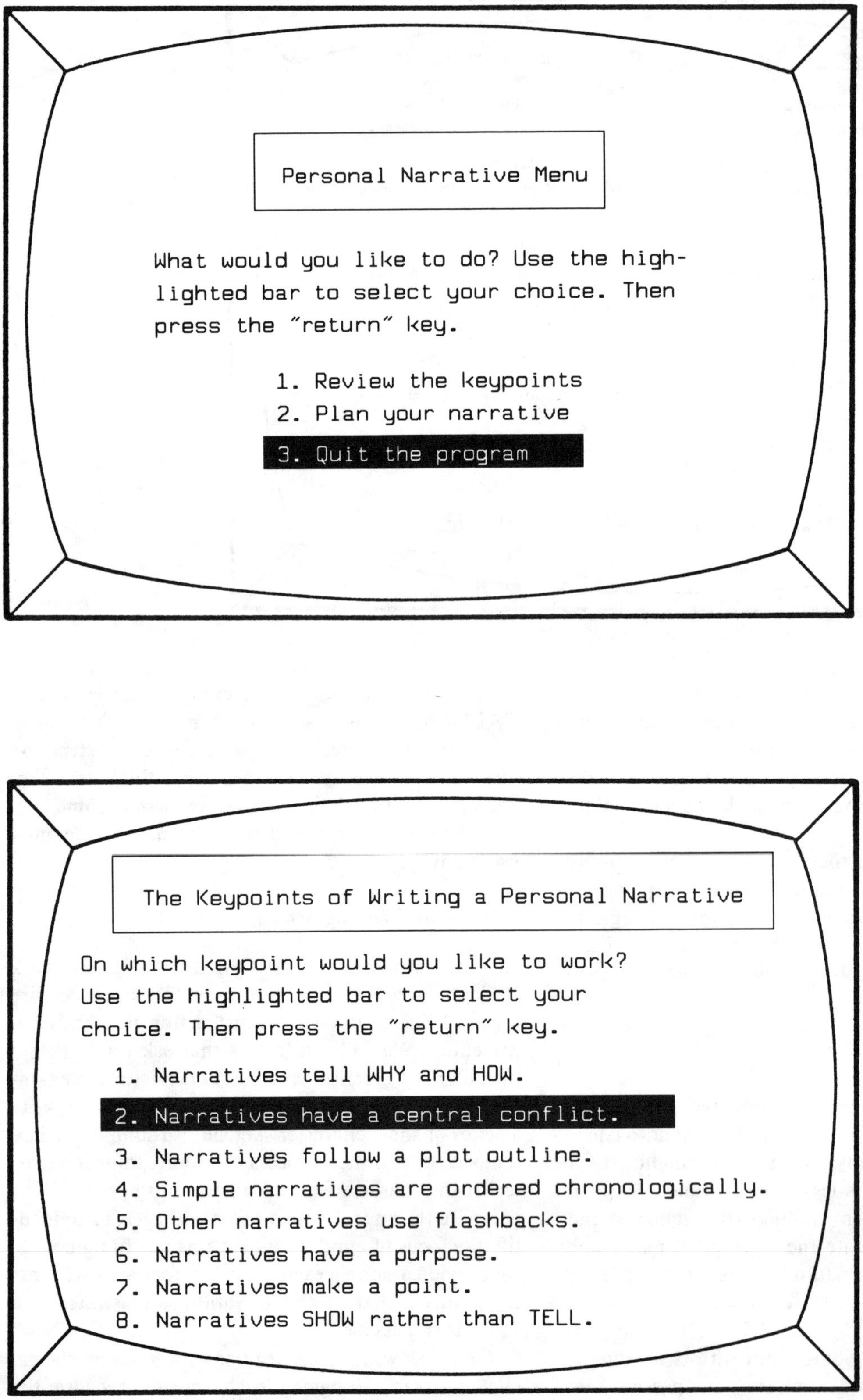

```
┌─────────────────────────────────────┐
│        Personal Narrative Menu       │
└─────────────────────────────────────┘

    What would you like to do? Use the high-
    lighted bar to select your choice. Then
    press the "return" key.

            1. Review the keypoints
            2. Plan your narrative
            █3. Quit the program█
```

```
┌──────────────────────────────────────────────────┐
│   The Keypoints of Writing a Personal Narrative    │
└──────────────────────────────────────────────────┘

   On which keypoint would you like to work?
   Use the highlighted bar to select your
   choice. Then press the "return" key.

        1. Narratives tell WHY and HOW.
       █2. Narratives have a central conflict.█
        3. Narratives follow a plot outline.
        4. Simple narratives are ordered chronologically.
        5. Other narratives use flashbacks.
        6. Narratives have a purpose.
        7. Narratives make a point.
        8. Narratives SHOW rather than TELL.
```

Figure 4.4: Sample Menu Screens

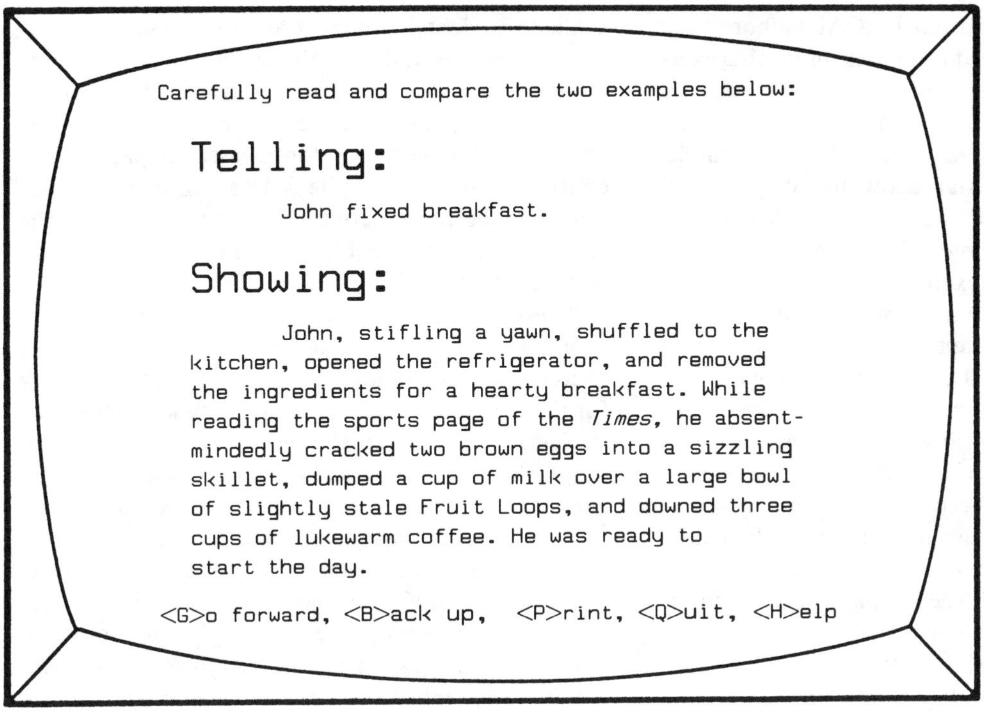

```
    Carefully read and compare the two examples below:

        Telling:

            John fixed breakfast.

        Showing:

                John, stifling a yawn, shuffled to the
        kitchen, opened the refrigerator, and removed
        the ingredients for a hearty breakfast. While
        reading the sports page of the Times, he absent-
        mindedly cracked two brown eggs into a sizzling
        skillet, dumped a cup of milk over a large bowl
        of slightly stale Fruit Loops, and downed three
        cups of lukewarm coffee. He was ready to
        start the day.

        <G>o forward, <B>ack up,  <P>rint, <Q>uit, <H>elp
```

Figure 4.5: Sample Instruction Screen

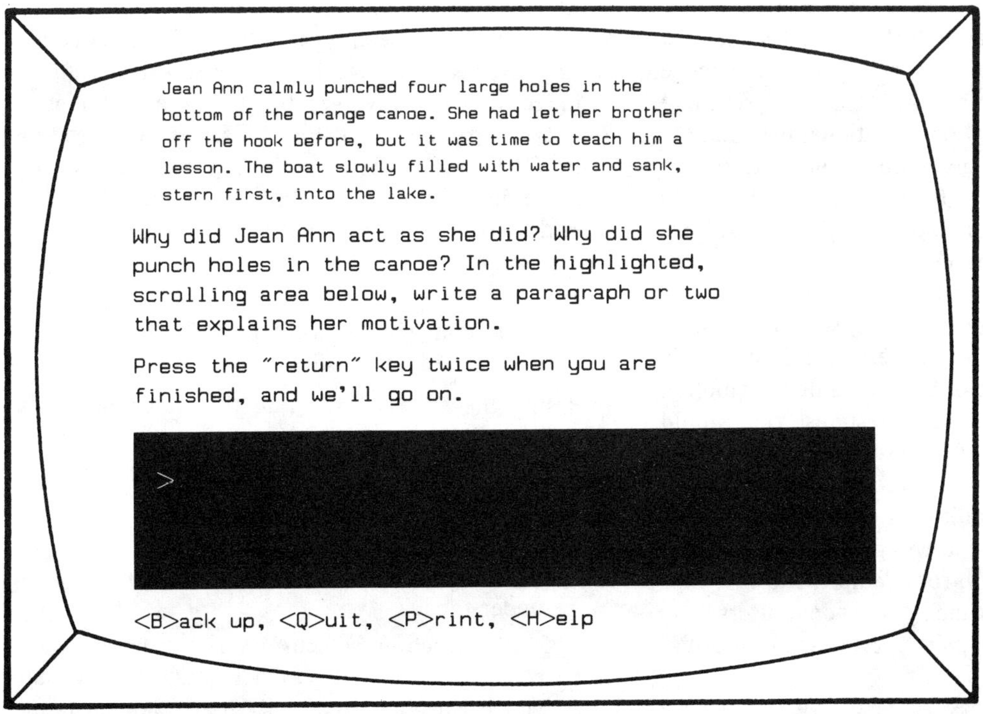

```
    Jean Ann calmly punched four large holes in the
    bottom of the orange canoe. She had let her brother
    off the hook before, but it was time to teach him a
    lesson. The boat slowly filled with water and sank,
    stern first, into the lake.

    Why did Jean Ann act as she did? Why did she
    punch holes in the canoe? In the highlighted,
    scrolling area below, write a paragraph or two
    that explains her motivation.

    Press the "return" key twice when you are
    finished, and we'll go on.

    >

    <B>ack up, <Q>uit, <P>rint, <H>elp
```

Figure 4.6: Sample Exercise Screen

long and complex. Traditionally, CAI authors have thought in terms of limited responses for writing exercises: one-letter, one-word, or one-sentence answers that can fit on the same screen with the question that prompts them. Figures 4.7 and 4.8, for example, represent two screens that allow for very limited responses on the part of users. However, teachers of composition often want much longer responses from their students in writing exercises: a paragraph, a ten-minute journal write, a lengthy brainstorming list, an audience analysis. In Chapter Six: Designing Screen Presentations for a CAI Lesson, we will suggest how composition teachers can work around the limitations of single-screen reponses for writing exercises.

Testing frames are special kinds of exercise screens. On such screens, the responses students give are subsequently used to evaluate their performance according to specific criteria identified in the lesson's instructional objectives. The testing screen in figure 4.9, for example, comes from a lesson on discourse aim. The lesson is designed to evaluate students' responses as "correct" if they match the entries on a teacher-designated list of appropriate answers that has already been programmed into the computer. Other examples of testing criteria might include asking students to list "at least five elements" to consider when analyzing a rhetorical situation, to identify "at least four kinds of cohesive ties" employed in a sample essay, to produce a paragraph that includes "at least seven out of ten vocabulary words," or to rearrange eight scrambled sentences so that "at least seven of them" follow a designated organizational pattern.

Because the answers given on testing screens are used to decide whether students have successfully completed an instructional objective, these screens determine how the program will branch in subsequent screens. If, for example, a student gives an unacceptable response on a testing screen, the CAI can branch to an appropriate message ("Not exactly the answer your teacher would have wanted, Ramon"), give more information about a response that would be acceptable ("You need to produce at least three *more* examples of summative modifiers"), and cycle the student through additional instruction and/or practice screens before proceeding with the remainder of the lesson. Figure 4.10, for example, shows a CAI screen designed as a branch for student users who provide an inappropriately short response to a journal-writing assignment.

The most difficult task associated with creating testing screens is figuring out how the computer can evaluate students' responses to an exercise as acceptable or not acceptable. If the testing criteria are simply measured ("explore your response to this story in a journal write lasting at least five minutes," "list at least ten possible topics for a research paper on a controversial issue," "write at least ten lines of prose that describe the experience"), this task is easy. The computer is quite capable of timing the duration of a writing activity and counting items.

However, in CAI destined for the writing classroom, a method for testing students' responses on an exercise screen cannot always be defined so simply for the computer. You may, for example, want to ask students to summarize the plot of a story in a paragraph that they are to compose. Because computers cannot read and understand such a response, you have to be inventive in identifying testing criteria that the computer *can* measure. In this case, for instance, you could identify for the computer a list of key words that an appropriate paragraph would contain. You could then ask the computer to search the student's paragraph response "for at least five words" that match this list. Using another approach to inventive evaluation, you could also provide a sample of an acceptable paragraph response and ask students to check their own work—a tactic best reserved for older or more highly motivated users.

One way of applying the information we have just provided you on screen types and assuring the quality of the screens you have already begun to design in your script draft involves filling out a systematic, quality-control checklist for each screen type used in your CAI lesson. In the following paragraphs you will see how Jean might have filled out a similar checklist for the instructional screens in her freewriting lesson.

Example of Controlling the Quality of Lesson Screen Types

Using the scale below, rate the statements that follow: 5 = very satisfied, 4 = mostly satisfied, 3 = can't decide, 2 = mostly dissatisfied, or 1 = very dissatisfied.

Total number of Instructional Screens   208

 __5__ Instruction screens are clear and easy to understand.

 __2__ Instruction screens are interspersed with exercise screens to provide students with an active learning situation. (Goal: Plan no more than two instruction screens in a row.)

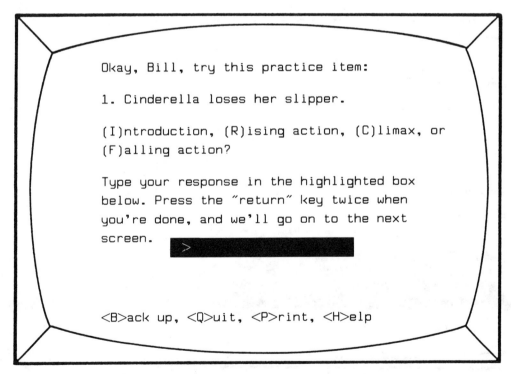

Here is the first example:

   DECEASED: Julia Haarmala, 49, of
Toivola, Michigan, died of leukemia at 8:00
p.m. on October 19, 1983, in Portage Lake
Hospital. Friends can send contributions to
the American Leukemia Foundation.

   Okay, Pat, was this piece written to
<I>nform, <P>ersuade, <A>muse, or <E>xpress
personal feelings? The piece may have a
combination of more than one aim or purpose.
Type in the letter(s) identifying the aim(s) or
purpose(s) of this writing on ONE line, and press
the "return" key to go on to the next screen.

<B>ack up, <Q>uit, <H>elp, <P>rint

Figure 4.7: Sample of Limited-Response Exercise Screen

   Okay, Bill, try this practice item:

1. Cinderella loses her slipper.

(I)ntroduction, (R)ising action, (C)limax, or
(F)alling action?

Type your response in the highlighted box
below. Press the "return" key twice when
you're done, and we'll go on to the next
screen.   >

<B>ack up, <Q>uit, <P>rint, <H>elp

Figure 4.8: Sample of Limited-Response Exercise Screen

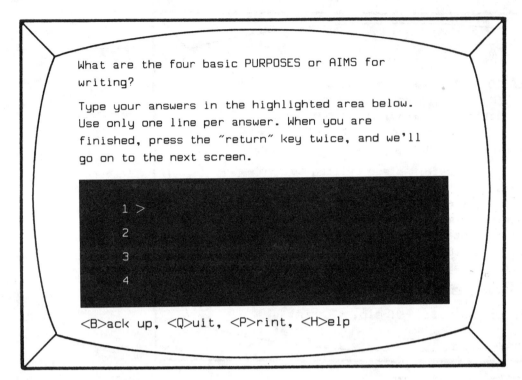

Figure 4.9: Sample Testing Screen

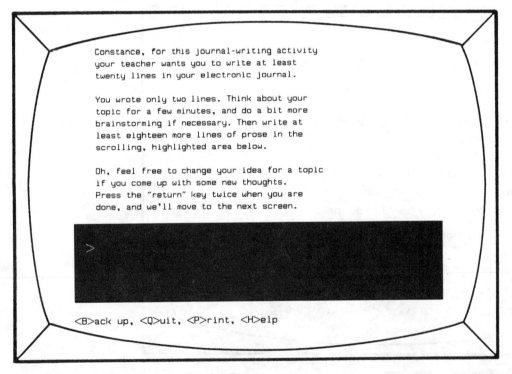

Figure 4.10: Sample Branch for an Inappropriate Response

__4__   Complicated instruction screens have optional help screens associated with them for students who become confused.

Notes: From looking at the notes for my script, I see that I have far too many passive instructional screens and not enough exercise screens. I also have too many instructional screens one right after the other. I want to try to break up these sets in future drafts of the script.

At the end of this chapter, you will find Worksheet 15: Controlling the Quality of Lesson Screen Types. This worksheet will encourage you to read over the first draft of your script and fill out a short quality-control checklist for each of the different screen types you have included in it. You can turn to this worksheet now, or read the remainder of this chapter first to get an overview of the remaining pedagogically oriented review tasks we will be asking you to do.

Considering Pedagogical Approaches in a CAI Lesson

In addition to writing instructional objectives and thinking about the various types of screens to use in a CAI lesson, authors also need to make decisions about the general pedagogical approaches to take in presenting the content of such a lesson. Authors must decide, for example, how to structure a lesson and choose an appropriate pedagogical approach for the students who will use the lesson. This section will briefly address these two major pedagogical issues and encourage you to think about them in relation to the particular CAI lesson you are planning.

Lesson Design

From experience, you know that writing instruction varies widely from teacher to teacher. Writing instruction that takes place on the computer is no different. Depending on a teacher's personality, teaching style, and the students he or she is addressing, an instructor may want to take advantage of one or more of the following lesson-design strategies in a CAI lesson.

Linear

Lessons based on a linear model represent the simplest and, therefore, the most common type of CAI now available. As figure 4.11 indicates, such lessons present every student with the same material in the

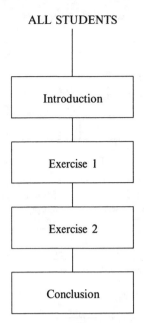

ALL STUDENTS

Figure 4.11: Map of a CAI Lesson Organized on a Linear Model

same sequence. Because students and teachers can become quickly bored with lessons designed in a linear fashion, this type of instruction is often criticized for having only a short useful life in a classroom or lab setting.

Although some experts feel that linear instruction may be appropriate for some of the simpler material presented in a writing course (drills on comma placement, vocabulary improvement, or spelling, for example), it is hard to justify its use for lessons that address more complicated, sophisticated, or abstract concepts involved in writing (e.g., invention, style, process).

Branching

CAI lessons that incorporate branching can allow students to take alternative routes through the instruction. As figure 4.12 illustrates, branching often occurs after a test screen: students who provide an appropriate response to such screens are sent along one instructional path, and students who give an inappropriate response are sent along a different path.

A CAI lesson, for example, can be designed so that it branches to provide different feedback messages for acceptable and unacceptable answers ("Well done, Alice . . ." or "I'm not convinced you understand, Don") or so that it branches to provide individualized instruction in the form of additional practice exercises, amplification of key terms, or challenging, extra-credit writing problems.

58   *Cynthia L. Selfe*

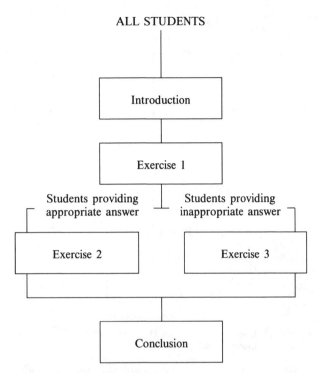

ALL STUDENTS

Figure 4.12: Map of a CAI Lesson Organized on a
Branching Model

If a teacher typically instructs students on two or three different levels of knowledge or sophistication, he or she might want to structure a CAI lesson so that it branches to different tracks or levels that remain consistently different throughout the lesson. Consider, for instance, a CAI unit on writing personal narratives. In such a unit, a teacher might want students on the highest track to work on longer writing assignments, consider more subtle distinctions of style, or try more difficult techniques of foreshadowing, ellipsis, or point of view. For those students who choose the middle or lower tracks, a CAI lesson can offer expanded explanations, shorter writing exercises, or additional outside reading.

Branching or tracking structures can also be useful for students who occasionally miss class. A CAI lesson can provide one pathway through the instruction that reviews material already presented in class and another pathway through the instruction for students who have attended class regularly.

Branching CAI lessons have both advantages and disadvantages when compared to linear CAI instruction. Because branching lessons require a great deal more planning and writing, they take more time and expertise to produce than do more simply structured

lessons. However, the structure of branching lessons often makes them more amenable to complex concepts in writing instruction and easier to adapt to most instructors' personal teaching styles.

Changing

CAI lessons can also be designed to change with every use. For example, *generative* programs can contain "banks" of prose samples, writing assignments, or instructional segments which are selected on a random basis. Every time such a lesson is used by a student, it will look different and provide new challenges. In figure 4.13 we have provided a screen that might be found in a generative lesson for a writing-intensive classroom.

Adaptive programs "learn" from the answers of every student who uses them. Such lessons, for example, could store students' critical evaluations of a paragraph and then use these evaluations to change or adapt the instructional material they present for future users. Figure 4.14 illustrates a screen that might be found in an adaptive lesson for a writing-intensive classroom.

CAI that changes for individual users, like CAI that branches, generally requires more planning and more time to produce than does linear instruction.

Lesson Approaches

To a great extent, personal teaching style can be reflected in the tone of a CAI lesson. If your writing instruction focuses on process rather than product, group work rather than lecture, discovery rather than rote learning, your CAI lesson can reflect this orientation. Below, we have suggested several distinct tones your CAI lesson can take.

Games

A game-like approach is especially suitable for lower grades, although many teachers of college students know how seductive computer games can be to young adults as well. In fact, the United States Air Force and Army have found computer games useful in their training of pilots. Games can be as challenging, as complicated, and as sophisticated as any other type of instruction, and, if you can accomplish your instructional objectives within a game-like lesson, your CAI might be all the more popular. Figure 4.15 provides an example of a screen that might be found in a game-like lesson for a writing-intensive classroom.

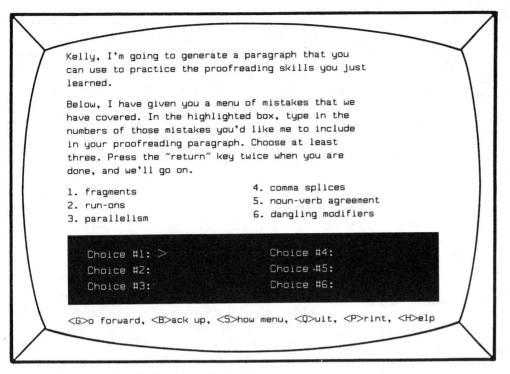

Figure 4.13: Sample Screen from Generative CAI Lesson

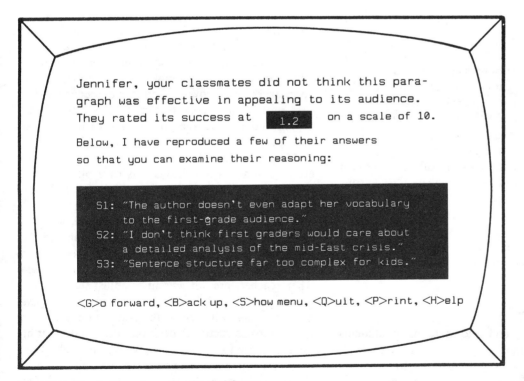

Figure 4.14: Sample Screen from Adaptive CAI Screen

Drill and Practice

This approach, sometimes referred to as the "electronic workbook," provides students with instruction and exercises on a certain topic. Generally, because this approach is most easily adaptable to a simple question-and-answer format (multiple-choice, fill-in-the-blank, short-answer) it is used to present basic material rather than more advanced or complicated concepts. Figure 4.16 provides an example of a screen that might be found in a drill-and-practice lesson for a writing-intensive classroom.

Some experts feel that the drill-and-practice approach has a place in composition classrooms because it can be useful for presenting instruction on topics like grammar, spelling, or reading comprehension. Other experts feel that this approach is actually harmful. They claim that drill-and-practice CAI focuses students' attention on minor, surface-level problems and takes away from the time they spend working on larger and more comprehensive problems such as invention, revision, or development.

Simulation and Problem Solving

Because computers can store great amounts of material, they are perfect for scenario, or simulated case-work, teaching. A technical writing instructor, for example, can write a CAI lesson that will present students with information about a mock company, its personnel, its correspondence, its products, its resources, and then set up a series of simulated communications problems that can be solved with this stored material. Figure 4.17 provides an example of a screen that might be found in a simulation-type lesson for a writing-intensive classroom.

If you enjoy using the problem-solving approach in teaching writing, you can also create CAI lessons that will guide students through the steps of solving a rhetorical problem and keep records of their progress at every point along the way. In figure 4.18, we show an example of a screen that might be found in a problem-solving lesson for a writing-intensive classroom.

Inductive or Deductive

CAI lessons can be constructed to move students inductively from examples to rules (called EGRUL instruction) or deductively from rules to examples (called RULEG). Figure 4.19 shows two screens, the first of which might be found in an inductively based lesson for a writing-intensive classroom and the second of which might be found in a deductively based lesson for a writing-intensive classroom.

If you are creating a CAI unit to cover a topic generally presented in a discovery-learning situation within your writing classroom, an inductive approach might be appropriate. For topics that you generally cover in a lecture situation, a deductive approach might be preferable.

Tutorial

Some teachers tend to confuse the tutorial approach with a drill-and-practice format, but carefully designed tutorial CAI can provide students with much more than a question-and-answer session. CAI built around the tutorial approach can contain, among other things, explanations of writing concepts at several different levels of sophistication or completeness, banks of student compositions which are analyzed or graded by teachers, descriptions of expert and novice composing strategies for specific writing assignments, and suggestions for getting started on writing problems. Figure 4.20 provides an example of a screen that might be found in a tutorial program designed for a writing lab.

Appropriateness

Creating CAI that will be of lasting value in a writing program or classroom necessarily involves a careful analysis of audience and teaching style. A teacher must consider, for example, what strategies and approaches have proven effective with students in the past or how the students' age, interest, and background might affect the presentation of a particular concept.

Most experienced teachers carry out these deliberations almost unconsciously as they plan or even conceive of a lesson. Then, they adjust the lesson presentation in the classroom as they see students' attention shift, as they sense impatience with an unnecessary explanation, or as they catalogue the misinterpretations that students share at the end of a lesson. However, because CAI is most often used when teachers are not present to adjust their presentations to such subtle cues, authors must *anticipate* how students will receive the instruction and then adjust the instructional decisions they make during field-testing efforts. (See Chapter Seven: Field Testing CAI for a more complete discussion of this topic.) Below, we have listed three important issues you may consider to help ensure the appropriateness of a lesson for a given population.

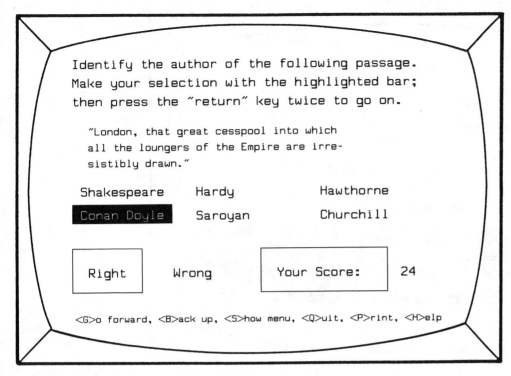

Figure 4.15: Sample Screen from a Game-Like CAI Lesson

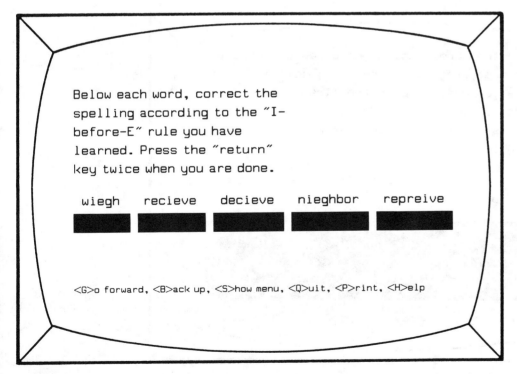

Figure 4.16: Sample Screen for a Drill-and-Practice Lesson

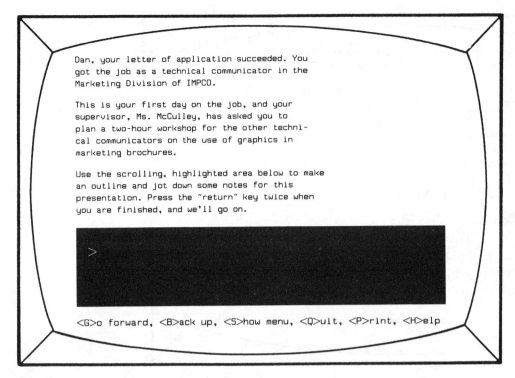

Figure 4.17: Sample Screen from a Simulation Lesson

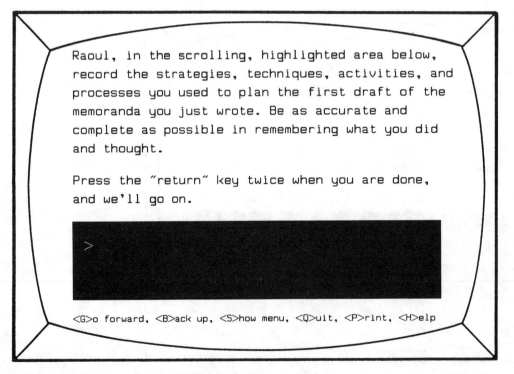

Figure 4.18: Sample Screen from Problem-Solving Lesson

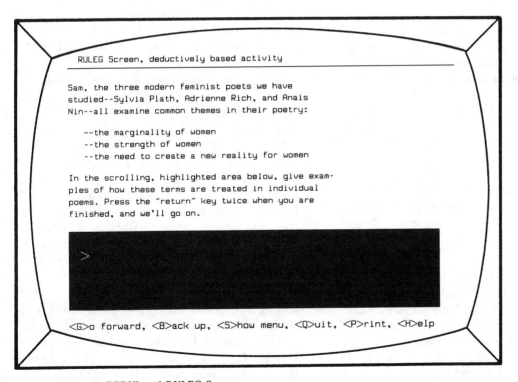

Figure 4.19: Sample EGRUL and RULEG Screens

Stylistic Appropriateness and Readability

Because the prose passages, directions, and sample essays contained in most writing-intensive CAI place heavy demands on the reading skills of students, it is best to analyze the stylistic characteristics that affect readability during the early design stages.

For authors who generate their scripts with the help of a computer and a word-processing program, this task can be made considerably easier and more systematic. Stylistic-analysis programs such as *Writer's Workbench* (Bell Laboratories) and *Grammatik* (Wang Electronic Publishing); or readability programs such as *Reading Level Analysis* (Berta Max, Inc.) or *Readability* (Micro Power and Light Company) should provide help in analyzing prose passages. If authors do not use a computer to help generate the material for their scripts, they can still apply traditional stylistic analyses or readability formulas to their work by hand.

Persona

The CAI lesson you create can employ any teaching persona you choose to invent. Some authors prefer a transparent persona, relatively free of personality. Figure 4.21, for example, shows a screen with a relatively transparent persona.

Other authors, however, prefer to employ a persona that shares their own sense of humor, concern for students' feelings, and enthusiasm for subject matter. Figure 4.22 shows a screen on which a definite persona is used by the author to simulate her own teaching style.

Still other CAI authors enjoy creating a persona that adopts an approach quite unlike their own in order to provide their students with a variety of instruction and approaches.

In any case, authors will want to make sure that the persona (or personae) they choose to create will appeal to their students and enhance rather than distract from the learning that is to take place.

Special Effects

Most microcomputers now offer a variety of special effects, and your main problem will be isolating those techniques that will help you accomplish your instructional objectives.

Special effects allow authors to emphasize certain words, sentences, or paragraphs on a screen through highlighting (also called reverse video), underlining,

flashing, or special character sets; to control the tempo of a lesson by presetting delays of a second or more between example questions and answers; or to capture the attention of students with graphic displays, animation, or scrolling text. In Chapter Six: Designing Screen Presentations, we will discuss these strategies further.

When a CAI lesson is field tested, authors should satisfy themselves that the special effects they have employed in their lessons do not distract students from accomplishing the instructional objectives they have defined.

To apply the information we have just provided about pedagogical approaches to your own CAI design effort, you may want to take some time to review your lesson plans and your script as they now stand. You will, of course, want to consider the basic design pattern of your lesson, the tone or approach you want to take, and the appropriateness of the material for the audience to which you will be aiming the lesson. In the following list, we show how Jean might have completed a similar task.

Example of Considering Pedagogical Approach

1. What design pattern (linear, branching, changing) does your lesson follow as it now stands? Given your assumptions about instruction, in general, and about writing instruction, specifically, what design pattern do you want your lesson to follow? Are revisions necessary? If so, what form will these revisions take?

   The lesson as it stands now is quite linear because I only have a skeletal outline of the main path through the material. What I want to add now is "side tracks," branches of the material designed especially for my advanced and slower learners.

2. What approach (game, drill-and-practice, simulation or problem-solving, inductive or deductive, tutorial) best describes your lesson as it now stands? Given your assumptions about instruction, in general, and about writing instruction, specifically, what approach do you want your lesson to follow? Are revisions necessary? If so, what form will these revisions take?

   As it now stands, the lesson is oriented around solving a particular writing problem by using free-writing techniques. So it is part problem-solving and part tutorial. I like this approach and want to keep the focus on a realistic writing problem even though I provide tutorial instruction as well.

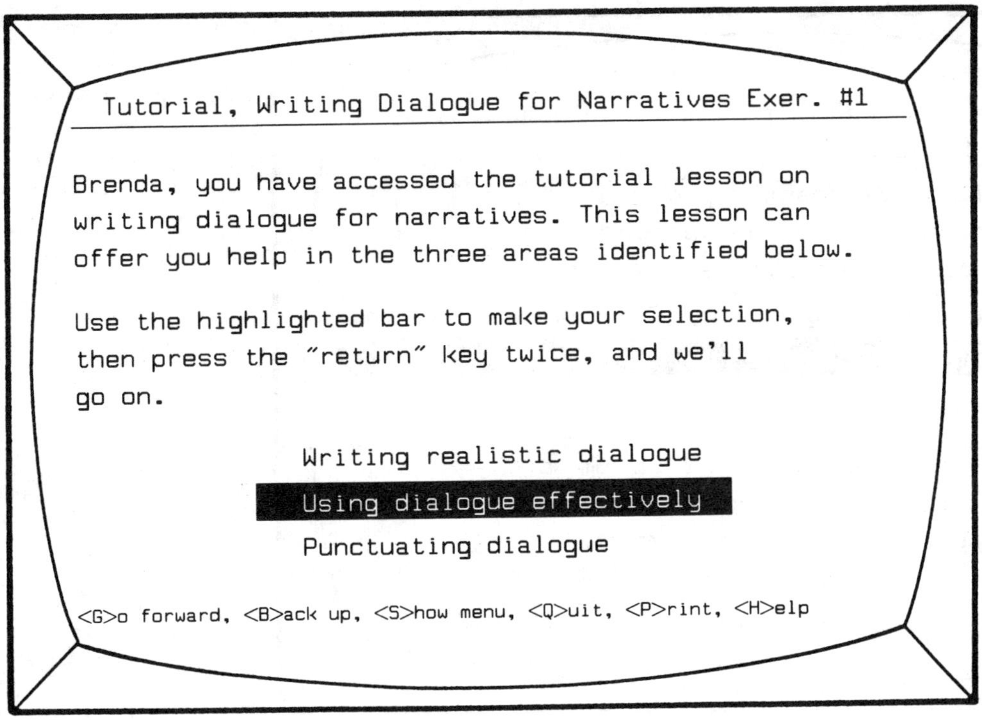

```
Tutorial, Writing Dialogue for Narratives Exer. #1

Brenda, you have accessed the tutorial lesson on
writing dialogue for narratives. This lesson can
offer you help in the three areas identified below.

Use the highlighted bar to make your selection,
then press the "return" key twice, and we'll
go on.

                Writing realistic dialogue
                Using dialogue effectively
                Punctuating dialogue

<G>o forward, <B>ack up, <S>how menu, <Q>uit, <P>rint, <H>elp
```

Figure 4.20: Sample Screen from a Tutorial CAI Lesson

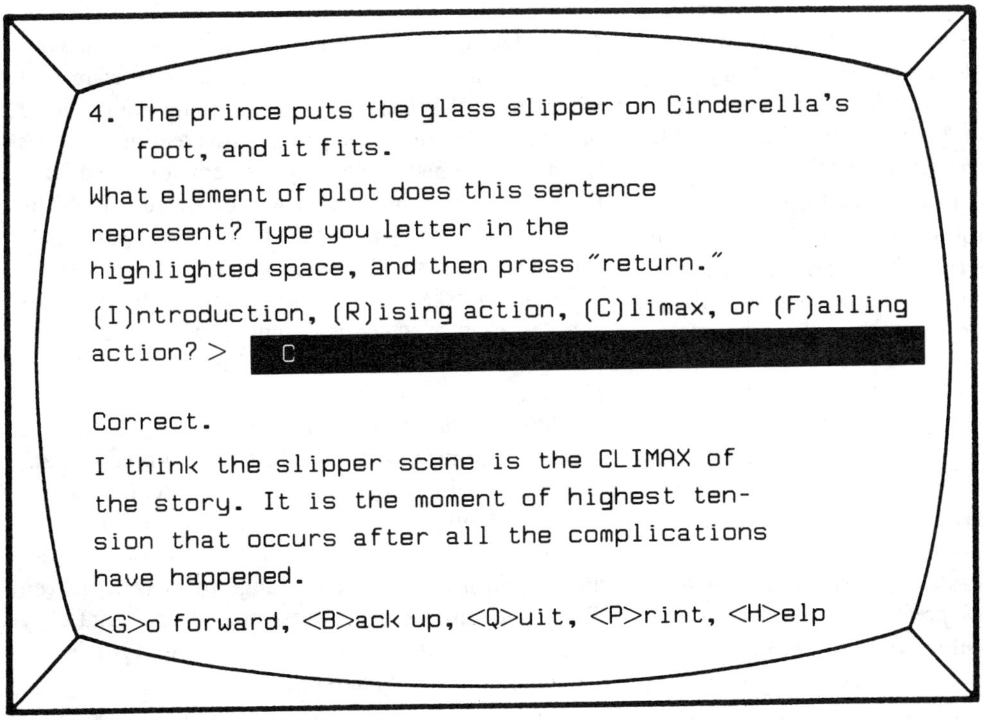

```
4. The prince puts the glass slipper on Cinderella's
   foot, and it fits.
What element of plot does this sentence
represent? Type you letter in the
highlighted space, and then press "return."
(I)ntroduction, (R)ising action, (C)limax, or (F)alling
action? >      C

Correct.
I think the slipper scene is the CLIMAX of
the story. It is the moment of highest ten-
sion that occurs after all the complications
have happened.
<G>o forward, <B>ack up, <Q>uit, <P>rint, <H>elp
```

Figure 4.21: Sample of Transparent Persona

```
 4. The prince puts the glass slipper on Cinderella's
    foot, and it fits.
 Can you tell me what element of plot this
 sentence represents? Type your letter in the
 highlighted space, and then press "return."
 (I)ntroduction, (R)ising action, (C)limax, or (F)alling
 action? >     C

 I agree, Pat.
 I think the slipper scene is the CLIMAX of
 the story. It is the moment of highest ten-
 sion that occurs after all the complications
 have happened.
 <G>o forward, <B>ack up, <Q>uit, <P>rint, <H>elp
```

Figure 4.22: Sample of Persona That Mirrors Teacher's Personality

3. Think once again about your targeted student audience. Are the style and reading level, the persona, and the special effects included in your lesson appropriate for them as it now stands? Do these elements directly support your assumptions about instruction, in general, and about writing instruction, specifically? Are revisions necessary? If so, what form will these revisions take?

Most of the activities I use in the lesson are taken right from my classroom, although there they are manifested in a more traditional form. If the activities are appropriate in my classroom—and I think, from observation, they are—then they should be fine for this lesson.

At the end of this chapter, on Worksheet 16: Considering Pedagogical Approaches, you can explore your thinking about the issues of lesson design, approach, and appropriateness much as we have explored Jean's thinking in the last example. Some readers may want to turn to this worksheet now and complete it. Others may prefer to read a few more chapters of this book before continuing their design efforts.

Summary

By the time you finish the tasks identified for this stage of CAI production, you will be well on your way to creating a valuable piece of courseware that will support the teaching in your writing classroom or program. Although the process of creating CAI, as we have outlined it here, may seem long and even tedious at times, its success will be demonstrated by your final product—a product that will be appropriate for your students and your classroom.

We have asked you to complete three tasks in this chapter, each of which is designed to help ensure the pedagogical soundness of the CAI lesson you are planning.

Defining the instructional objectives of CAI. This activity requires authors to identify, in a precise manner, those things they want students to be able to accomplish after using a particular CAI lesson.

Identifying screen types. This activity provides authors with exposure to a range of possible screen formats to use in a CAI lesson and asks that they think about how to use various screen types in the CAI lesson they are planning.

Thinking about lesson design, approach, and appropriateness. This activity reminds authors of three important issues involved in designing CAI that reflects their own personal teaching style and asks them to explore the impact these issues might have on the lesson they are planning.

In the next two chapters, we will explore more issues that will help you revise the first draft of your CAI script as you ready it for the programmer and educational specialist on your design team.

From experience, we can attest to the importance of refining your script as much as possible *before* it goes into program form. Changes at the later stage of programming are not only more costly, but much more time-consuming than those completed earlier.

Note

1. Many of the screens included in this chapter have been taken directly from WordsWork (a CAI program developed at Michigan Technological University by Dr. Billie Wahlstrom and me in connection with Michigan Tech Software) or suggested indirectly from my other work with Dr. Wahlstrom. For the permission to use the WordsWork screens, I thank Billie Wahlstrom, my coeditor; Tim Nelson, President of Michigan Tech Software; and Michigan Technological University. For the inspiration on the screens I have used indirectly, I thank Billie Wahlstrom also. We think so much alike that it is impossible to trace the exact ownership of our ideas.

Worksheet 14: Identifying Instructional Objectives

Before beginning this worksheet, review those topics and activities you identified in Worksheet 6: Completing a Task Analysis of a CAI Lesson and in the draft of your screen-by-screen lesson script. Make sure you have identified *all* of the concepts that you want to cover in connection with the stated purpose of your lesson. Revise or expand the original task-analysis list you compiled in light of this review.

In the spaces labeled "subtopic" below, fill in an item from the revised task-analysis list you have compiled. After each subtopic or activity you identify, list and number the instructional objectives associated with finishing that particular segment of instruction. Be as complete as possible, and make sure that each instructional objective contains a *context* for learning, an *action* that students must do, and *testing criteria* for evaluating the successful completion of the objective.

Subtopic: _____

    Objective _____

    Objective _____

    Objective _____

Subtopic: _____

    Objective _____

    Objective _____

    Objective _____

Worksheet 15: Controlling the Quality of Lesson Screen Types

For the activity described on this worksheet, you will need your rough draft of the screen-by-screen script for your CAI lesson.

Go through this screen-by-screen script and, in the top right-hand corner of each page, code the screen type using the following designations.

IS   Introductory Screens
OS   Orientation Screens
HS   Help Screens
INS Instruction Screens
ES   Exercise Screens
CS   Concluding Screens
____ Others

Use the scale below to indicate your satisfaction with how each screen type meets the criteria indicated.

5 = very satisfied
4 = mostly satisfied
3 = can't decide
2 = mostly dissatisfied
1 = very dissatisfied

1. Total number of IS   _____

_____ Mandatory introductory materials (those screens presented to every user) are brief enough to avoid frustrating students who access the CAI more than once.

_____ Mandatory introductory material is complete enough to provide students with the information they need to identify the lesson (author, publisher, copyright, title of lesson, title of series, etc.).

_____ Optional introductory screens (those that users can choose to select) provide sufficient explanation for students who may need further information about the lesson or how to use it.

_____ All introductory screens establish an appropriate tone for the remainder of the lesson.

Notes:

2. Total number of OS   _____

   _____ Mandatory orientation material is brief enough to avoid boring students who use the CAI more than once.

   _____ Optional orientation material is complete enough to inform a novice user of the important facts (length of lesson, placement in series, purpose, procedure).

   _____ All orientation material is clear and easy to understand.

   Notes:

3. Total number of HS   _____

   _____ Help screens are located in optional branches to avoid boring students who use the CAI more than once.

   _____ Optional help screens are complete enough to provide the information novice users need (explanations of cursor control, menu use, prompts, key strokes, etc.).

   _____ All help screens are clear and easy to understand.

   _____ Help screens are easy for students to find and access.

   Notes:

Worksheet 15 continued

4. Total number of menu screens   _____

  _____ Menu screens are clear and easy to understand.

  _____ Menu screens are easy to use.

  _____ Menu screens do not confuse students by asking them to route themselves through too many layers or branches of the program at one time. (Goal: plan no more than three different menu screens in a row.)

  _____ Complicated menu screens have optional help screens associated with them for students who become confused.

  _____ Menu screens accurately reflect the structure of the lesson.

Notes:

5. Total number of INS   _____

  _____ Instruction screens are clear and easy to understand.

  _____ Instruction screens are interspersed with exercise screens to provide students with an active learning situation. (Goal: plan no more than two instruction screens in a row.)

  _____ Complicated instruction screens have optional help screens associated with them for students who become confused.

Notes:

Worksheet 15 continued

6. Total number of ES   _____

_____ Exercise screens are clear and easy to understand.

_____ Exercise screens contain clear, concise directions. They give students all parameters necessary for succeeding on exercises. (Examples: where on the screen to respond, when to respond, how long response should be, time limits for a response, nature of response, etc.)

_____ Complicated exercise screens have optional help screens associated with them for students who become confused.

Notes:

7. Total number of CS   _____

_____ Concluding screens are clear and easy to understand.

_____ Concluding screens give students clear directions for finishing the lesson. (Examples: what to do with the writing produced as a result of the lesson, how to get a hard copy of their writing or how to store it in their own files / disks, what lesson to access next, how to get off the computer, where to put lesson materials, when to check in with a teacher or tutor.)

_____ Complicated concluding screens have optional help screens associated with them for students who become confused.

Notes:

Worksheet 15 continued

Worksheet 16: Considering Pedagogical Approach

To complete this worksheet, you need a draft of the screen-by-screen script for your CAI lesson and copies of the work you did for Worksheet 2: Identifying Assumptions about Writing, Worksheet 3: Identifying Assumptions about Teaching Writing, and Worksheet 7: Determining the Context for a CAI Lesson.

Review your work on each of these documents, and then answer the questions below.

1. What design pattern (linear, branching, changing) does your lesson follow as it now stands? Given your assumptions about instruction, in general, and about writing instruction, specifically, what design pattern do you want your lesson to follow? Are revisions necessary? If so, what form will these revisions take?

2. What approach (game, drill and practice, simulation and problem-solving, inductive or deductive, tutorial) best describes your lesson as it now stands? Given your assumptions about instruction, in general, and about writing instruction, specifically, what approach do you want your lesson to follow? Are revisions necessary? If so, what form will these revisions take?

3. Think once again about your targeted student audience. Are the style and reading level, the persona, and the special effects included in your lesson appropriate for them as it now stands? Do these elements directly support your assumptions about instruction, in general, and about writing instruction, specifically? Are revisions necessary? If so, what form will these revisions take?

5 INTEGRATING RESPONSE AND EVALUATION INTO A CAI LESSON

In the last chapter, we suggested some pedagogical issues to think about in connection with your CAI lesson and discussed how to revise the first draft of a screen-by-screen script in light of these deliberations. In the next few pages, we continue to explore CAI from a pedagogical point of view—this time with an eye toward the responses, those made by both students and teachers, that will be a part of your lesson. The first part of this chapter discusses the two major kinds of responses that a CAI lesson can include and outlines the advantages and disadvantages of each. The second part of the chapter discusses the ethical issues involved in evaluating students' responses to writing activities in a CAI lesson.

Responding to Student Input

In the most basic sense, there are two ways to respond to the material students type on the computer screen when answering questions, writing assignments, and completing activities in a CAI lesson.

1. The lesson can provide *answer-specific responses* that will trigger certain types of feedback (and/or evaluation) based on the words or phrases students type into the computer.

2. The lesson can provide *open-ended responses* that will not provide feedback specific to students' input.

Answer-Specific Responses

Although answer-specific responses to students' input are desirable because they help individualize instruction, they are also more difficult to incorporate in a lesson and are limited by the intelligence of computers in general. Answer-specific responses are created by anticipating and listing the entire range of "correct" answers students could give in any particular situation and then programming the computer to match this list against actual student input. If the computer finds

a match (or a specified number of matches), the student input is given a "correct" response. If there is no match or only a partial match, an "incorrect" or "partially correct" response is given.

A teacher could, for instance, use an answer-specific activity in asking students to identify the theme of a paragraph. In constructing this activity for a CAI lesson, the composition specialist would have to first, choose an appropriate paragraph and state the theme of this passage in his or her own words; next, compile a list of key words and phrases that *could* be included in a "correct" identification of this theme, including on this list as many synonyms, near synonyms, dialect and slang rephrasings as possible; then, stipulate, for a programmer, exactly which combinations of these terms or how many of these terms *must* be included in an answer for it to be deemed "correct."

As you might guess, this type of response is much easier to compose for questions that require simple answers—answers that don't vary widely, that consist of one letter, one word, or a specified number of items that are easily counted. The answer-specific screen represented in figure 5.1, for instance, asks students to type in the number of journal entries they have completed since their last session on the computer. For the exercise on this screen, a "correct" answer has been defined by the teacher/author as five or more entries. Unfortunately, not all student responses to questions and not all writing assignments in a process-based composition classroom are as easy to define or anticipate.

The advantages of answer-specific responses are tantalizing for authors who are creating their own CAI. If such responses are constructed carefully, they can provide different feedback for appropriate, inappropriate, and partially appropriate answers. For example, an answer-specific response could match a student's answer against a list of anticipated "correct" answers constructed by the teacher. If a student's response *did not match* the requisite item or number of items on the "correct" list, the lesson would branch to a series of screens that explain the problem and suggest extra practice. Figure 5.2, for example, shows a screen from a lesson on brainstorming that might be appropriate for a student who offers a response that does not match one on the "correct" list. If the answer *did match* appropriate items on the "correct" list, the lesson would branch to a series of screens that would offer praise, additional instruction, or more challenging activities. The screen in figure 5.3, for instance, might be an appropriate follow-up frame for a student whose response was identified as correct. If the student's response was *a partial match,* the answer-specific activity could branch to a series of screens that would ask for rephrasing or further elaboration. In figure 5.4, we provide an example of a screen that could be used for a student's partially correct response in a brainstorming lesson.

There are also disadvantages connected to answer-specific responses, however. Because it is almost impossible to anticipate *all* the acceptable or unacceptable answers to a question (particularly those subtle and complex questions that seem to abound in writing-intensive classrooms), answer-specific responses sometimes result in inappropriate feedback which frustrates or confuses students. In figure 5.5, for instance, you can see a screen from a lesson on nutshelling that provides inappropriately positive feedback to a student's incorrect answer. The teacher who defined "correct" and "incorrect" answers for this activity did not anticipate the problem of students who had not attended class or heard the initial lecture on nutshelling.

Dr. Billie Wahlstrom, coeditor of WordsWork (a series of process-based CAI lessons for composition classrooms), tells a story about the problems associated with answer-specific responses. In one lesson, Wahlstrom wanted students to read a paragraph about a young woman breaking up with her boyfriend and give their interpretation of the main character's motivation. Although Wahlstrom tried to anticipate key words in every possible "correct" answer students might give—compiling a "correct" list of more than thirty-five words such as *mad, angry, jilted, break up, out of love, stepping out,* etc.—the first student to field test the software got an "incorrect" response to a "correct" answer because he used an unanticipated phrase—*pissed off.*

Some experts feel that the difficulty involved in anticipating acceptable responses for answer-specific CAI may encourage authors to deal with simplistic questions and answers and, further, that it may limit the use of these responses in writing instruction that addresses more complex rhetorical concepts. There are, however, any number of answer-specific activities that work well in a process-oriented composition classroom. As long as answer-specific screens are based on current research, theory, and pedagogy in the field of composition, they can serve a valuable function in a CAI lesson destined for writing-intensive classrooms. We suggest experimenting with answer-specific responses in appropriate situations throughout a CAI lesson and observing the strengths and weaknesses of individual questions during the field testing of your CAI lesson.

Open-Ended Responses

Open-ended responses offer alternatives to answer-specific responses. Open-ended responses give the same message to users, regardless of the answer or the material they provide. Open-ended responses do not require CAI authors to compile lists of "correct" answers against which student input can be evaluated. Open-ended responses, however, do create activities that ask or encourage students to evaluate their own input. On the screen represented in figure 5.6, for instance, students are asked to identify the revising strategy that seems most valuable to them. The response to this input is open-ended. Regardless of the strategy typed in, the screen tells students to take their printouts for use in a later tutoring session.

There are certain advantages to using open-ended responses. Like answer-specific responses, they can include models of correct answers. Figure 5.7, for example, shows an open-ended response screen that identifies the three characteristics of a correct answer and encourages students to evaluate their own work. In addition, open-ended responses, because they are not dependent on anticipating the content of a student's input, never give inappropriate messages. Rather, they encourage students to make their own responsible decisions about how to proceed through the lesson—whether they need more practice, further explanation of a concept, or increased challenge.

Because open-ended responses do not evaluate students' input, they may be particularly suitable for writing instruction for two reasons. First, questions or activities that employ such responses encourage the risk-taking that writing teachers often value. In a private conversation with a CAI lesson that is non-judgmental, students may feel free to try out new and unfamiliar writing styles or techniques. Second, open-ended activities may be particularly suitable to composition instruction because they can allow students

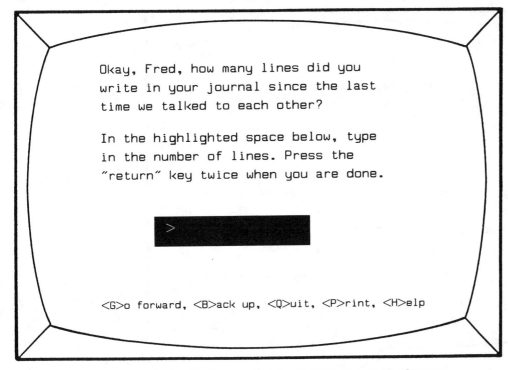

Figure 5.1: Example of an Answer-Specific Response That Can Be Easily Evaluated by Computer

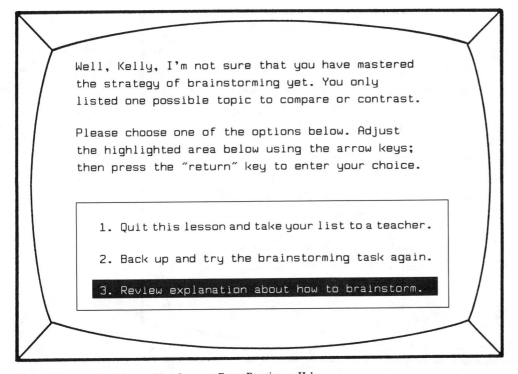

Figure 5.2: Example of Screen That Suggests Extra Practice or Help

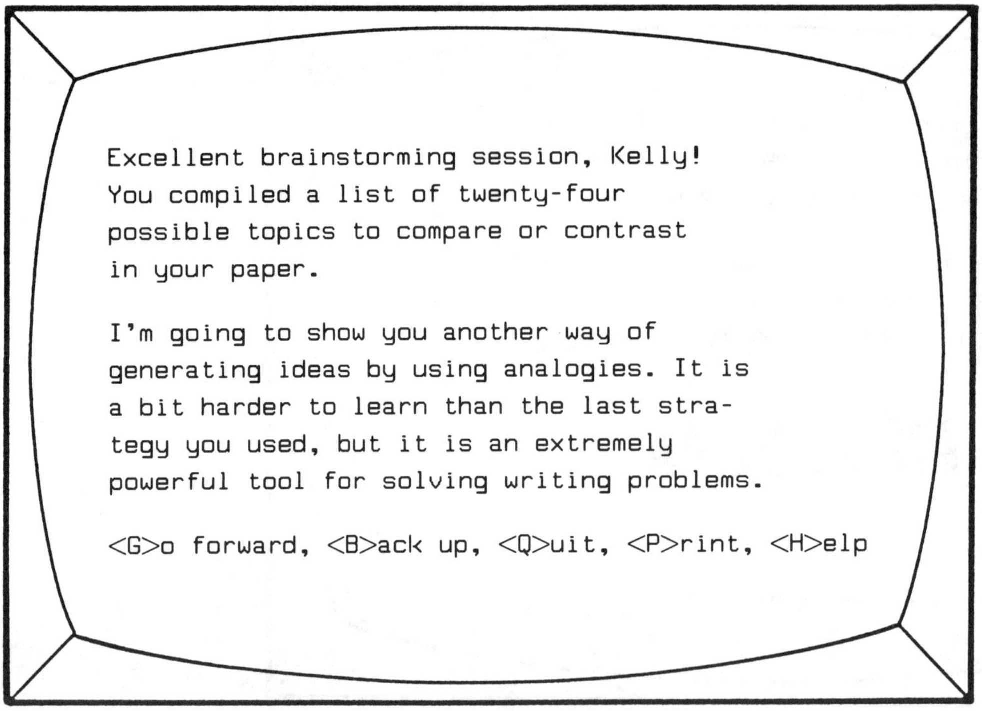

```
Excellent brainstorming session, Kelly!
You compiled a list of twenty-four
possible topics to compare or contrast
in your paper.

I'm going to show you another way of
generating ideas by using analogies. It is
a bit harder to learn than the last stra-
tegy you used, but it is an extremely
powerful tool for solving writing problems.

<G>o forward, <B>ack up, <Q>uit, <P>rint, <H>elp
```

Figure 5.3: Example of Screen That Branches to More Challenging Instruction

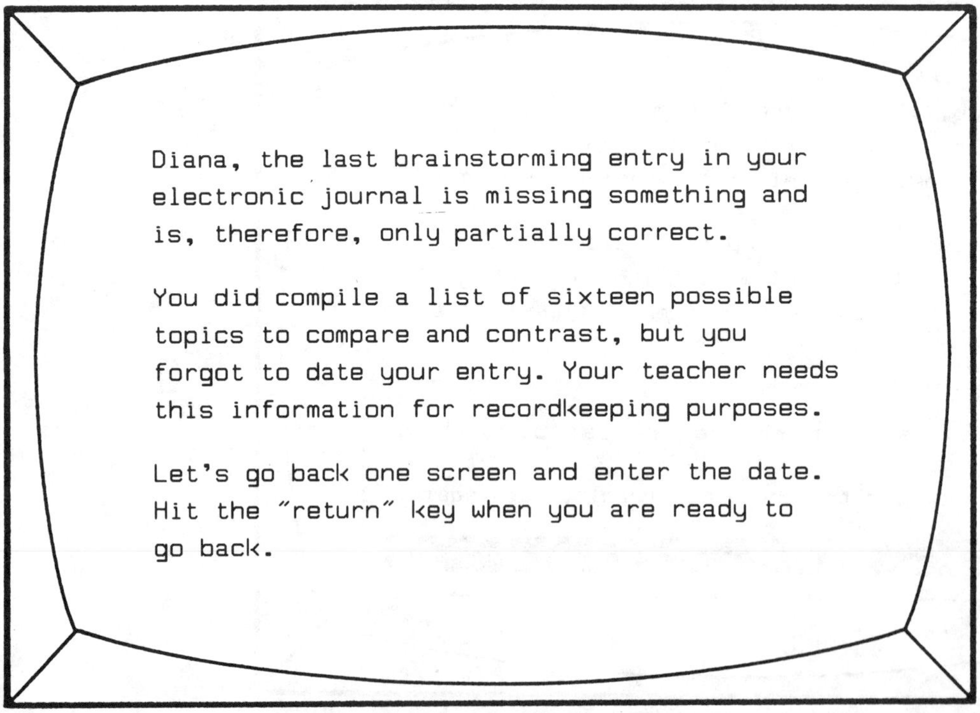

```
Diana, the last brainstorming entry in your
electronic journal is missing something and
is, therefore, only partially correct.

You did compile a list of sixteen possible
topics to compare and contrast, but you
forgot to date your entry. Your teacher needs
this information for recordkeeping purposes.

Let's go back one screen and enter the date.
Hit the "return" key when you are ready to
go back.
```

Figure 5.4: Example of Answer-Specific Response to a Partially "Correct" Answer

```
Margaret, in the space below, identify the theme
of your paper in one sentence. This activity is
a form of the "nutshelling" strategy.

Press the "return" key twice when you are done,
and we'll go on.

  I don't know what nutshelling is! I must have

  missed that part of the lesson for this paper.

Great, Margaret. The one sentence you typed
in the highlighted area is a very concise
statement of your theme.

Now let's go on to other revising activities.

<G>o on, <B>ack up, <Q>uit, <H>elp, <P>rint
```

Figure 5.5: Example of an Inappropriate Response to an Answer-Specific Item

```
Ron, we're near the end of this lesson on revising.

In the highlighted area below, identify the
revising strategy that has proven most helpful
to you. Tell why this strategy is so effective.

When you're done, hit the "return" key twice,
and I'll print what you've written.

  >

Good job, Ron. Now, take this printout with you
next time you go to the Reading/Writing Center.
You can discuss it with your tutor.

<G>o on, <B>ack up, <P>rint, <Q>uit, <H>elp
```

Figure 5.6: Example of an Open-Ended Response Screen

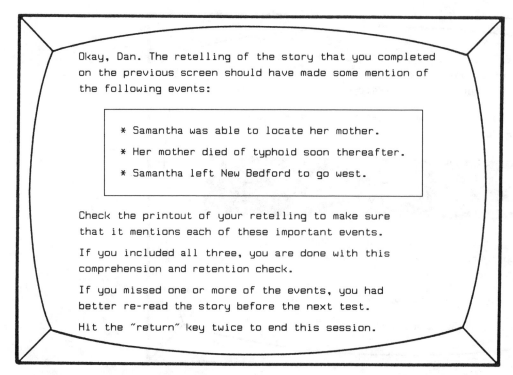

Figure 5.7: Example of Open-Ended Response Screen That Models a Correct Answer for Students'
Self-Evaluation Effort

to find their own way through a writing problem, to follow their own thinking patterns to a logical conclusion.

If we believe currently accepted language theories which indicate the act of writing—*in and of itself*—is a way of thinking about a subject, it follows that open-ended responses can be used when we want to avoid limiting or artificially directing creative problem solving at early stages of the writing process. For example, open-ended responses might best be employed when we want to leave students alone, to let them find their own way through a writing problem, to discover—as they struggle to manipulate observations and to encode their thoughts logically in a linguistic symbol system—what they are thinking about a topic. In these cases, teacher-focused, answer-specific evaluation may be constraining.

These very advantages, however, suggest related disadvantages. Open-ended responses, because they frequently rely on student judgment or interpretation, are subject to abuse. Younger or less serious students may see open-ended responses as tempting opportunities to sabotage instruction or may simply fail to understand the importance of being rigorous in comparing their answers to the appropriate models provided by the teacher. Moreover, because activities

designed to use open-ended responses are not constructed to "recognize" the appropriateness of student input, they provide what some teachers consider limited information for grading purposes. This criticism, however, may not necessarily be valid. Examine, for instance, the open-ended response screen represented in figure 5.8. It is true that this screen is not designed to send any information to the teacher's recordkeeping file on whether the student provided an appropriate or inappropriate answer—only the student will judge this. However, even with this open-ended response the author can structure the activity so that the computer automatically records for the teacher the length of the student's answer (words, lines, sentences, paragraphs), the time it took to write, and the number of times the student attempted that activity. The machine can also list the additional practice the student attempted and print out the response for later use in a teacher-student conference.

As you think about the material we have just presented on open-ended responses, you may want to examine and critique individual open-ended response screens that you have already designed for the first draft of your screen-by-screen script. What follows is a checklist that should prove valuable for these critiques. We have completed it as Jean might have for

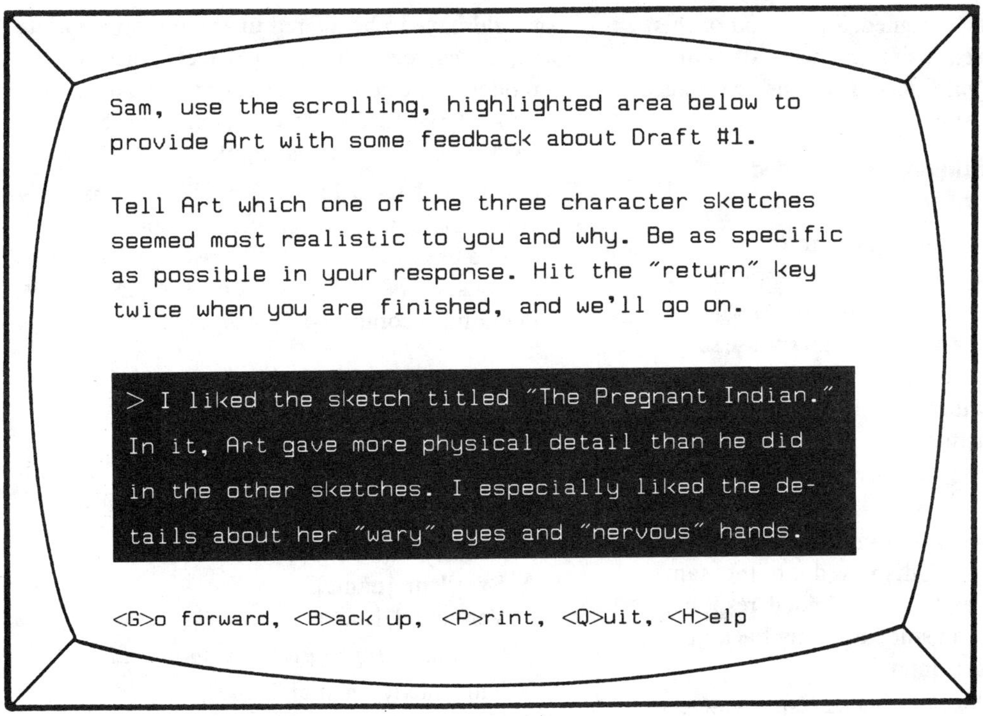

```
Sam, use the scrolling, highlighted area below to
provide Art with some feedback about Draft #1.

Tell Art which one of the three character sketches
seemed most realistic to you and why. Be as specific
as possible in your response. Hit the "return" key
twice when you are finished, and we'll go on.
```

> I liked the sketch titled "The Pregnant Indian."
In it, Art gave more physical detail than he did
in the other sketches. I especially liked the details about her "wary" eyes and "nervous" hands.

```
<G>o forward, <B>ack up, <P>rint, <Q>uit, <H>elp
```

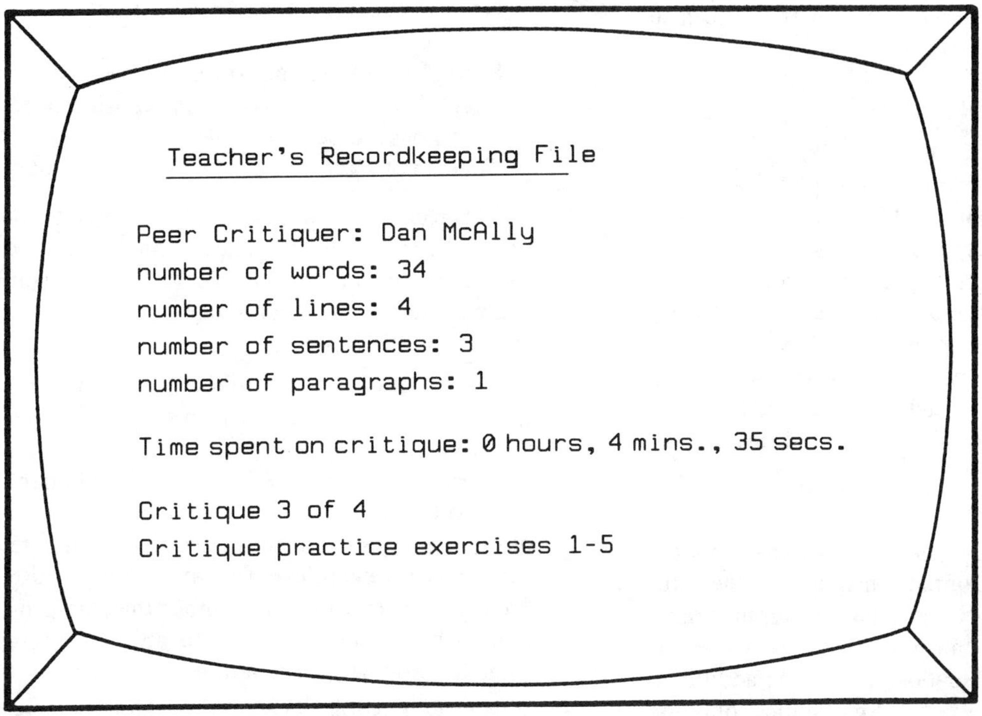

```
Teacher's Recordkeeping File

Peer Critiquer: Dan McAlly
number of words: 34
number of lines: 4
number of sentences: 3
number of paragraphs: 1

Time spent on critique: 0 hours, 4 mins., 35 secs.

Critique 3 of 4
Critique practice exercises 1-5
```

Figure 5.8: Open-Ended Response Screen and Recordkeeping Data Sent to Teacher's File

an open-ended screen she designed. At the end of this chapter, we have provided a similar checklist, Worksheet 17: Critiquing Open-Ended Response Screens, for use with your own script.

Example of Critiquing Open-Ended Response Screens

(YES) NO   Does this open-ended response screen require a model of an "appropriate" response? If so, is one provided?

(YES) NO   Does this open-ended response screen require students to identify the appropriateness or the inappropriateness of their own answers? If so, are students given clear criteria for evaluating their responses?

YES (NO)   Can students' input to this particular activity be displayed on the same screen as this open-ended response? If not, can students easily back up to view their input?

(YES) NO   Does this open-ended response screen tell or suggest to students what to do next?

Notes: Provide a "model" answer on an optional help screen so that students can refer to it if they don't immediately understand the evaluation criteria I give on this screen in an abbreviated form.

Scripting Responses

If you, or your design team, has completed a screen-by-screen script of your CAI, you have already sketched out the kinds of responses the computer should make to students' input for each activity. In light of the material in the preceding section, however, you may want to go back over the screen-by-screen lesson script and revise the responses you have identified. Below, we have included five suggestions for revising scripting responses. At the end of this chapter you will have the opportunity to apply these guidelines to your own script.

1. Always provide a model or explanation of a "correct" or appropriate answer, whether students provide appropriate, partially appropriate, or inappropriate answers themselves or not. These model explanations can act as additional instruction. In figure 5.9, for instance, only the last two words in the first line of the screen would have to be altered to make it appropriate for a "correct" or an "incorrect" answer. The model of the "correct" answer that takes up the bulk of the screen would remain the same regardless of the students' input.

2. Create and label lists of appropriate, partially appropriate, and inappropriate responses which can be used throughout the lesson. Notice these response lists that Jean, our sample teacher, might have composed.

Examples of Scripting Answer-Specific Responses

"Appropriate" Response List (ARL)
Good job, [name].
Your answer is correct.
[Name], that's right.
Excellent, [name].
Very good, [name].
"Partially Appropriate" Response List (PRL)
Not exactly, [name].
You've got it partially correct.
I only recognize part of your answer, [name].
At least one part of your answer is correct, [name].
"Inappropriate" Response List (IRL)
No, [name], I do not recognize that answer as correct.
Sorry, [name], that answer is incorrect.
[Name], your teacher does not consider that response to be acceptable.
That is not right.

This technique can add variety to the instruction. At the end of this chapter, on Worksheet 18: Scripting Answer-Specific Responses, you will have the opportunity to construct your own answer-specific response lists.

3. Use a standard set of symbols to describe responses in your screen-by-screen script. We have illustrated one way of labeling responses in figure 5.10. Notice that line 2 uses bracketed directions to tell the programmer to choose any one of the responses from the Appropriate-Response List (ARL). Regardless of what system you use for labeling responses, remember that the programmer on your team must be able to understand and follow your notations.

4. Whenever possible, keep the student's answer on the screen along with the response you give.

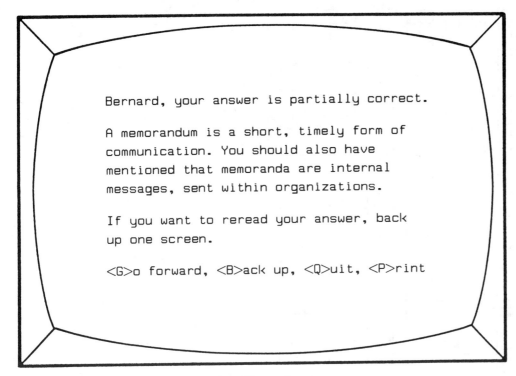

```
Bernard, your answer is partially correct.

A memorandum is a short, timely form of
communication. You should also have
mentioned that memoranda are internal
messages, sent within organizations.

If you want to reread your answer, back
up one screen.

<G>o forward, <B>ack up, <Q>uit, <P>rint
```

Figure 5.9: Example of Screen with Explanation of Correct Answer

The screen in figure 5.11, for instance, is efficiently designed to ask students a question; accept their input in the scrolling, highlighted area; and provide an open-ended response by the teacher—all on the same frame. When it is not possible to arrange everything you want on the same screen, make sure that students can back up and review their answers in light of the response you have given. The screen depicted in figure 5.9, for example, provides students the opportunity of "backing up" in the instructional sequence by moving to the choice line at the bottom of the screen and pressing the letter "B."

5. Whenever possible, on the same screen as a response, tell students what to do next or ask them what they would like to do next. The screen response in figure 5.12, for example, tells students who provide inappropriate answers that they will undertake an additional practice exercise on the "I-before-E" spelling rule. The screen depicted in figure 5.13 asks students to decide for themselves if they require additional practice on the spelling rule. Whichever approach you choose, provide clear directions to keep students from becoming confused.

As you think about the guidelines we have just presented on response screens, you may want to review and rewrite some of the response frames you have already designed for the first draft of your own screen-by-screen script.

Response and Evaluation

Whatever method a CAI lesson employs to respond to student input—answer-specific responses, open-ended responses, or a mixture of both—it must have some way of evaluating student performance and reporting the results of this evaluation. Evaluation, however, especially in connection with writing, can be a complex issue, involving a number of ethical decisions. On the following pages, we have tried to anticipate some of the questions authors might have about evaluating students' input in a CAI lesson.

Why Evaluate Students' Written Work in a CAI Lesson?

There are several reasons. First, because students often use CAI outside the classroom, without the benefit of a teacher's presence, evaluation serves the

Example of Labeling Response Inserts

Screen Description: Instructional, Appropriate Response

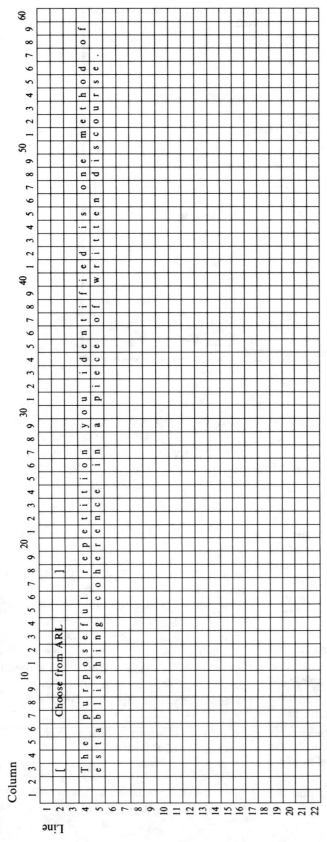

Figure 5.10: Labeling Responses in Script by Referring to Response Lists

```
What is the biggest strength of your draft as it
now stands, Dan? In the highlighted space below,
identify this strength in a one-sentence nutshell.
Hit the "return" key twice when you are finished.

   > I like the pro-feminist argument I set up.

     It is almost fully developed at this point

     although I might be able to add one more

     really effective example to wind it up.

Okay, Dan. Think about this strength. How can you
capitalize on it in your next draft? When you are
ready to answer this question, go on to the next
screen.

<G>o forward, <B>ack up, <Q>uit, <P>rint
```

Figure 5.11: Example of Teacher's Response on the Same Screen as Student's Input

```
Choose the correct spelling from the choices
below. Use the arrow keys to move the high-
lighted box around the correctly spelled word.
Then press the "return" key twice to go on.


   recieve        riceive      receive      recive


No, Dorie. The correct spelling is RECEIVE.
Let me provide you with more practice on
the "I before E" rules. Hit the "return" key
when you are ready, and we'll go on.
```

Figure 5.12: Teacher's Directions on the Same Screen as Student's Response

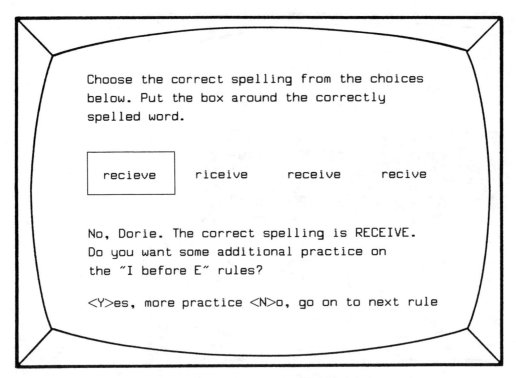

Figure 5.13: Example of Screen That Allows Students to Determine Direction of Instruction

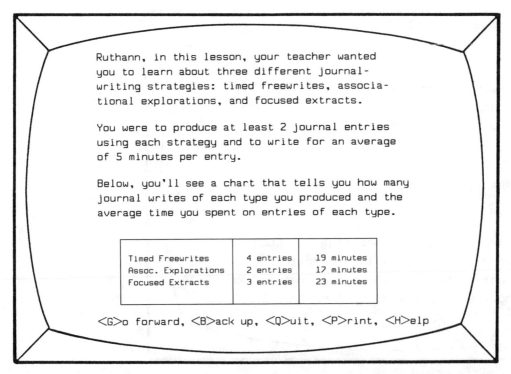

Figure 5.14: Example of Screen That Identifies Students' Performance on Instructional Objectives

important function of providing some way of judging success in learning. A good evaluation system will apprise student users of their progress and give them a realistic idea of how they have performed on the instructional objectives identified by the teacher as the basis for the lesson. The screen represented in figure 5.14, for instance, identifies not only the lesson's instructional objectives ("learn about three different freewriting strategies: timed freewrites, associational explorations, and focused extracts"), but also the criteria for judging success on these objectives (". . . produce at least two journal entries using each strategy . . . write for an average of five minutes per entry"), and students' individual performance data for self-evaluation purposes.

Second, building evaluation into a CAI lesson makes it possible to individualize instruction by varying the material students will receive according to the appropriateness or inappropriateness of their input. Without some form of evaluation, either student- or teacher-based, there would be no way to determine when a student should receive additional instruction, or when a program should branch to further explanations, practice activities, enrichment material, or writing assignments.

Third, if a system of evaluation is carefully planned (if such a system is related directly to instructional objectives and based on a teacher's assumptions about teaching in general and teaching writing specifically), it can help authors judge the effectiveness of a CAI lesson. For instance, each of the instructional objectives you identified earlier for your CAI lesson (Worksheet 14: Identifying Instructional Objectives) outlined specific criteria for evaluating student success. If you also build a system of recordkeeping into your CAI (one that sends information to the teacher's file describing every student's performance on each of the instructional objectives you have identified), you can determine which lesson activities are most consistently effective in teaching those concepts you consider important and which activities need revising because they are ineffective in their instructional approach. In this sense, evaluation can also help you in revising and field testing a CAI lesson. We will discuss more about field-testing strategies in Chapter Seven: Planning a Field-Testing Program for a CAI Lesson.

When Should Students Be Evaluated in a CAI Lesson?

Each of the instructional objectives authors identify for a CAI lesson should have some method of evalu-

ating student progress attached to it. If this caveat is followed, the author can evaluate student progress continually, with each activity and concept presented. However, timing is crucial in determining the *type* of evaluation to use. Let's look, for example, at an instructional objective that Jean might have used for her CAI lesson on freewriting.

Example of Identifying Instructional Objectives

Given instructional screens that explain what timed freewriting and brainstorming are and given a short narrative writing assignment, students will be able to brainstorm a list of at least fifteen possible topics.

In this activity, Jean's purpose is to expose students to the concepts of timed freewriting and brainstorming and to make sure they try these prewriting strategies in a realistic setting. At this early point in the composing process, Jean would probably want to emphasize creative, imaginative thinking. She would not want to encourage her students to turn on their internal "editors" too early. This central goal, then, would determine her evaluation plan—having the computer simply *count* the number of items on the brainstorming list. As the sample objective indicates, she would not include in this evaluation effort any attempt to determine the quality of the ideas that students listed, accurate spelling, grammatical correctness, or even appropriateness for the writing assignment. Although these evaluation activities might be appropriate in other lessons or activities that Jean might plan later, the prewriting period is, most likely, not the time to include them.

How Can I Evaluate Students' Input?

The *purpose* of each instructional objective within a lesson should determine the form and structure of evaluation. Some objectives might be best evaluated in terms of quality ("Is this paper ready to be read by your peer group?"), others in terms of simple quantity ("How many times have you rewritten this paper?"). Performance on some objectives might best be evaluated by the students themselves. Students, for example, might be the best judges of whether they need more practice writing memoranda or if they need more time to explore an interesting paper topic. Other objectives might be best evaluated by the teacher. In these cases, CAI authors can anticipate "correct" or appropriate answers and have the computer compare student input with this list.

As you read over the list of instructional objectives that you compiled on Worksheet 14: Identifying Instructional Objectives, think about whether any of the following methods of evaluation might be appropriate:

Counting

Computers can count almost anything: time, words, phrases, sentences, transitions, lines of prose, passive constructions, adjectives, practice exercises, etc. The successful accomplishment of some objectives can be evaluated simply by counting the number of things a student types on the screen. The screen represented in figure 5.15, for instance, was designed for an instructional objective that judged users' success on a revision activity by counting entries.

Matching

Computers can match student input against "correct" or appropriate answers anticipated by a teacher. This matching function permits fill-in-the-blank questions, short-answer questions, or multiple-choice questions to be evaluated. Some essay-length questions can also be evaluated in a limited sense using this method. A CAI author could, for example, construct a list of key words or phrases that an appropriate essay answer should contain and search students' input for a specified number of these words or phrases. The screen in figure 5.16 illustrates this kind of "matching" strategy for essay questions. The author of this screen has written an essay question to be answered by student users in the scrolling highlighted area and has provided a "matching" list of appropriate answers and directions for the team programmer on how to employ this list in the program for evaluating students' success.

Modeling

A lesson can provide students with an appropriate or an inappropriate model and ask them to compare it to their own version in specified ways. As demonstrated in figure 5.17, a teacher could, for example, provide a stylistic analysis of three authors' works as models, ask students to analyze their own styles, and then ask them to compare the results for themselves. If such activities are constructed carefully, models do not have to be narrowly prescriptive.

Discussing

Students' success on certain instructional objectives might best be evaluated by a teacher, a tutor, or a peer. A CAI lesson can give students directions to consult any of these individuals for feedback on specific activities. The screen depicted in figure 5.18, for example, directs students to take the hard copy they have produced during a CAI lesson on letter writing and exchange it with classmates for a peer critique.

What Do I Do with Evaluation Information?

Once a teacher has evaluated students' performances on an instructional objective, what can or should be done with the information? Again, the purpose of the instruction should influence this decision. If timely evaluation information is important for a student's progress in a lesson (rather than for a teacher's recordkeeping purposes), a CAI author can choose to display the evaluation information on the computer screen as students finish individual activities within a longer lesson, without sending such data to a teacher's recordkeeping file. The screen in figure 5.19, for instance, might appear for the students' benefit at the end of a short lesson segment on reducing wordiness that exists within a longer lesson on style. In other cases, an author may want to have evaluation information printed out in a tabular form at the end of a full lesson. Figure 5.20 shows an example of students' performance data as presented in a table at the end of an entire lesson on proofreading.

If evaluation information is important for a *teacher* to see, a CAI author can choose to send students' performance data automatically to a recordkeeping file for periodic review by the instructor or have it printed out for students to bring to their next conference with the teacher. The screen in figure 5.21, for instance, represents data from a proofreading lesson that has been stored in a tabular form within a teacher's recordkeeping file.

Authors of CAI lessons should realize that their decisions about *where* to send evaluation information will directly affect the way in which students approach a CAI lesson, just as similar decisions affect student performance in a traditional instructional setting. Students might, for example, feel less inclined to take chances with their writing or to try new techniques and strategies if they know that their attempts will be scrutinized and evaluated by a teacher. Often students are attracted to CAI because they can take risks without worrying about another human seeing their writing; if you value this kind of activity, you may want to honor the privacy of the student-computer relationship by denying any access to material written during a CAI session.

Objective: After practicing 5 revision strategies, students will be able to identify at least 2 appropriate strategies to use in revising a draft of a paper they produce.

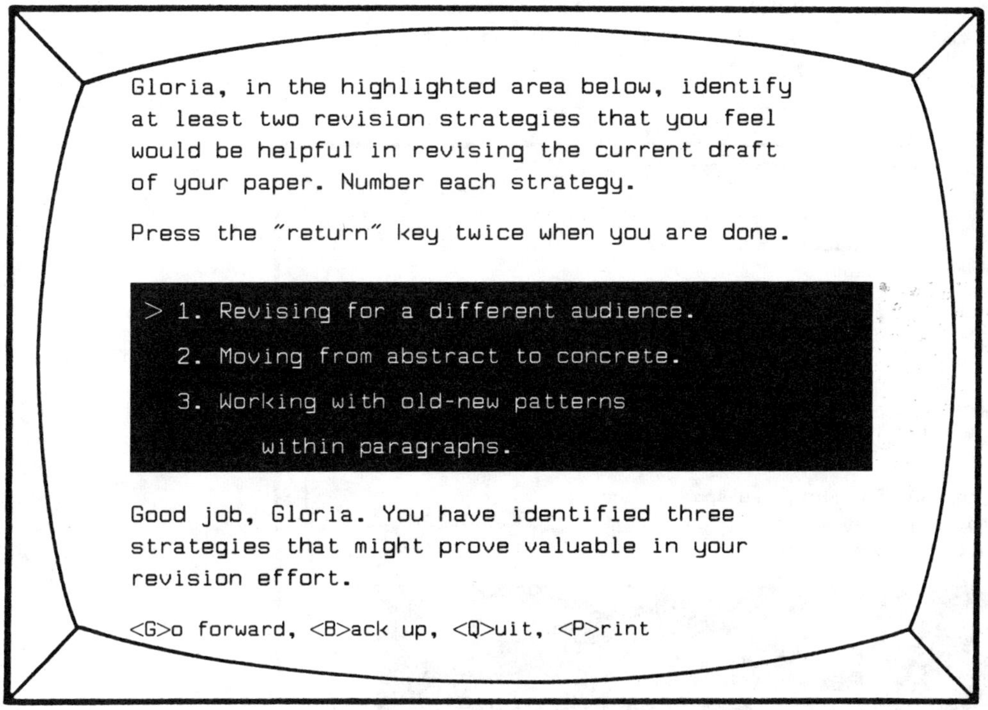

```
Gloria, in the highlighted area below, identify
at least two revision strategies that you feel
would be helpful in revising the current draft
of your paper. Number each strategy.

Press the "return" key twice when you are done.

    > 1. Revising for a different audience.

      2. Moving from abstract to concrete.

      3. Working with old-new patterns

             within paragraphs.

Good job, Gloria. You have identified three
strategies that might prove valuable in your
revision effort.

<G>o forward, <B>ack up, <Q>uit, <P>rint
```

Figure 5.15: Instructional Objective That Can Be Evaluated by Counting

In some lessons, teachers may prefer to let students choose what to do with the written material they generate via computer and the evaluation information generated in a CAI session. The screen depicted in figure 5.22, for instance, asks students to determine the ultimate destination of their written drafts. The author of this screen was content with suggesting various possibilities for feedback and leaving the final decisions up to student users. In other lessons, teachers may want to keep closer tabs on student performance. If you *do* choose to have material sent automatically to a teacher's file or to a peer's file, be sure to inform students at appropriate points throughout the lesson that the material they write will become public property.

After reading the material we have just presented on evaluation, you may want to review and rethink the evaluation approaches you use on certain screens in your own CAI script. The following list shows how Jean might have completed such a review, using the worksheet we provided for this purpose.

Example of Reviewing Evaluation Approaches

Activity: Timed freewriting, practice #1

1. Are the evaluation instructions for this activity clear for the programmer? Is a standard set of symbols used to designate responses for appropriate, partially appropriate, and inappropriate input?

   Check out labeling conventions with the consultant. See if we can decide on a numbering system for the screens.

2. Is the method of evaluation—counting, matching, modeling, discussing—in accord with the purpose of the instructional activity? Am I evaluating *what* I want to evaluate in the *way* it should be evaluated?

   Might have too many "counting" evaluations. I notice that I evaluate most journal entries by counting the number of lines—that doesn't give enough information about content of students' entries—try modeling good answers and

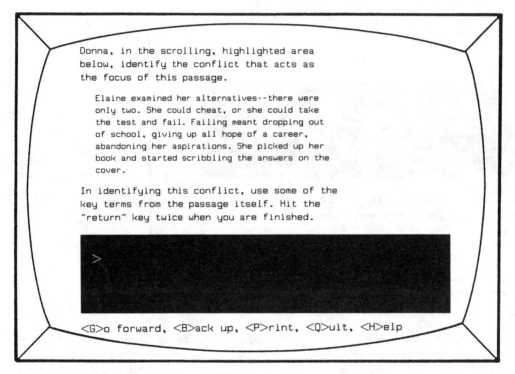

Figure 5.16: Identifying a List of "Appropriate" Matches for Student Input

letting them evaluate their own entries on some activities.

3. What kinds of evaluation information will result from this activity? A table listing the number of "correct" or "incorrect" answers? A count of elapsed writing time? A hard copy of a writing assignment? What form will this information take?

For each journal entry, I want a count of the number of lines and words written, a measure of the elapsed writing time, and some indication of how pleased the writer is with the effort.

4. Where is the evaluation information sent? To teachers? Students? Is this decision consistent with the purpose of the instructional objective connected to this activity?

I want the entries themselves to remain private so that students will take some chances in their thinking. I do want some data on entry length, time spent, etc.

At the end of this chapter, on Worksheet 19: Reviewing Evaluation Approaches, we will provide the opportunity for you to think about evaluation approaches in a format similar to the one you have just seen. Some readers may want to turn to this worksheet now and begin the process of reviewing their approach to evaluation. Others may want to continue reading before they proceed with their review.

Summary

This chapter covered some of the issues connected to responses—both teacher and student responses—in a

```
Terry, here are the results of our study on adjective use.

        ┌─────────────────────────────────────────────────────────┐
        │  Terry's Draft   Authors    #1    #2    #3    #4         │
        │  S1      4                   5     4     3     2         │
        │  S2      3                   3     1     2     8         │
        │  S3      3                   7     4    11     6         │
        │  S4      2                   5     5     3     3         │
        │  S5      1                   2     1     6     4         │
        │  S6      3                   5     4     3     2         │
        │  S7      6                   3     1     2     8         │
        │  S8      5                   4     4     3     3         │
        │  S9      5                   2     2     2     1         │
        │  S10     2                   3     5     1     4         │
        │  S11     3                   2     3     8     7         │
        │       ─────                ─────────────────────        │
        │  Avg.  3.3          Avg.  3.7   3.1   4.0   4.7          │
        └─────────────────────────────────────────────────────────┘

Given our previous discussion of adjective use, can you draw any
conclusions from this data? Hit the "return" key twice to go on to
the next screen.
```

Figure 5.17: Example of a Model That Is Not Narrowly Prescriptive

```
Doug, you have reached the end of this
lesson on writing effective business
letters.

Take the draft of the letter that you
have produced to the next meeting
of your Technical Writing class.

Exchange letters with one member of
your critique group, and then revise
it before letting the entire critique
group comment on it.

<G>o forward, <B>ack up, <Q>uit, <H>elp, <P>rint
```

Figure 5.18: Example of Screen That Encourages Students to Discuss Their Work with Peers

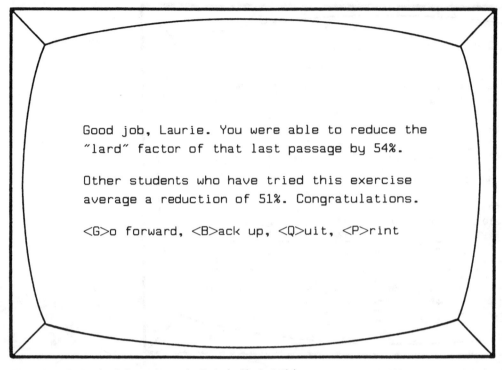

Figure 5.19: Evaluation Information at the End of a Single Activity

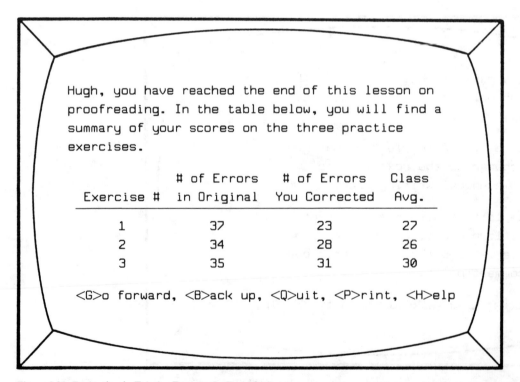

Figure 5.20: Evaluation in Tabular Form at the End of a Lesson

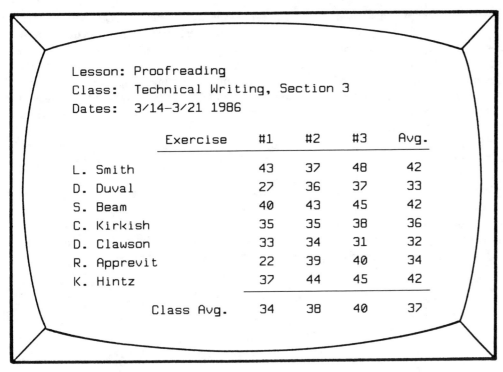

```
Lesson: Proofreading
Class:  Technical Writing, Section 3
Dates:  3/14-3/21 1986

             Exercise    #1    #2    #3    Avg.
             _____
L. Smith                 43    37    48    42
D. Duval                 27    36    37    33
S. Beam                  40    43    45    42
C. Kirkish               35    35    38    36
D. Clawson               33    34    31    32
R. Apprevit              22    39    40    34
K. Hintz                 37    44    45    42
             _____
         Class Avg.      34    38    40    37
```

Figure 5.21: Examples of Teacher's Recordkeeping File

```
Suzette, choose one of the options below by
moving the highlighted area with the arrow
keys. When you have marked your choice,
press the "return" key twice to enter your
selection.

Send this draft to my tutor's file for
      our next session.

Send this draft to my teacher for grading.

Send this draft to my peer-critique group
      for written feedback.

Send this draft to my private file.
```

Figure 5.22: Screen That Lets Students Decide What to Do with Written Material

CAI lesson. The first part of the chapter discussed two different ways to respond to student input.

The use of answer-specific responses requires authors to anticipate and create a list of "correct" or appropriate answers to lesson questions; tell the computer to check student input against this list for full, partial, or negative matches; and provide a bank of appropriate messages for each kind of match. Answer-specific responses are advantageous because they individualize instruction. These items are, however, difficult to construct because they rely on the teacher's ability to predict a complete and accurate list of "correct" or appropriate variations for an answer.

Open-ended responses do not use a system of scanning student answers and matching them against a list of "correct" answers. Rather, these responses give the same message to all students regardless of their input. Open-ended questions are advantageous because they allow students to assume the responsibility for determining whether their answers are appropriate, partially appropriate, or inappropriate. Open-ended responses may not always be suitable for younger or less motivated users because they rely on students' judgment.

In connection with these two basic kinds of responses, we also listed five suggestions for scripting responses.

The second part of this chapter discussed questions that authors of CAI lessons might have had about evaluating student responses: *why, when,* and *how* to evaluate students' written work, and *what* to do with evaluation information.

Worksheet 17: Critiquing Open-Ended Response Screens

To complete this worksheet, you need a copy of the latest screen-by-screen draft of your CAI script. Go through the script, and identify each of the activities for which you want to provide *open-ended* responses. Then, for every open-ended response you have planned, answer the following questions.

YES	NO	Does this open-ended response require a model of an "appropriate" response? If so, is one provided?
YES	NO	Does this open-ended response require students to identify the appropriateness or the inappropriateness of their own answers? If so, are students given clear criteria for evaluating their responses?
YES	NO	Can students' input to this particular activity be displayed on the same screen as this open-ended response? If not, can students easily back up to view their input?
YES	NO	Does this open-ended response tell or suggest to students what to do next?

Worksheet 18: Scripting Answer-Specific Responses

To complete this worksheet, you need the latest draft of your screen-by-screen lesson script. Go through the script, and mark every activity that requires an *answer-specific* response to student input. Then, finish the four tasks we outline on this worksheet, and use the answer-specific response lists you create to revise the screen-by-screen script as needed. Be sure to employ a standard set of symbols or labels in the script to let a programmer know what kind of response is needed.

1. Create a list of responses for appropriate or "correct" answers.

"Appropriate" Response List (ARL)

2. Create a list of responses for partially appropriate or partially "correct" answers.

"Partially-Appropriate" Response List (PRL)

3. Create a list of responses for inappropriate or "incorrect" answers.

"Inappropriate" Response List (IRL)

4. Create and label a list of miscellaneous responses for use in special situations.

"Miscellaneous" Response List (MRL)

ex. MRL1 Please think of at least [number] more topics.

MRL2 [name], if you want further help on this concept, go see a tutor or your teacher.

MRL3 [name], go back to the last screen, reread the directions, and try again.

Worksheet 19: Reviewing Evaluation Approaches

To complete this worksheet, you need the latest draft of your screen-by-screen lesson script. Go through this draft, and identify each activity which involves an evaluation of student input. Using a copy of this worksheet for each activity, answer the questions listed below.

Activity:

1. Are the evaluation instructions for this activity clear for the programmer? Is a standard set of symbols used to designate responses for appropriate, partially appropriate, and inappropriate input?

2. Is the method of evaluation—counting, matching, modeling, discussing—in accord with the purpose of the instructional activity? Am I evaluating *what* I want to evaluate in the *way* it should be evaluated?

3. What kinds of evaluation information will result from this activity? A table listing the number of "correct" or "incorrect" answers? A count of elapsed writing time? A hard copy of a writing assignment? What form will this information take?

4. Where is the evaluation information sent? To teachers? Students? Is this decision consistent with the purpose of the instructional objective connected to this activity?

6 THINKING ABOUT SCREEN DISPLAY

A piece of instruction that appears on a computer screen, simply by virtue of being displayed via an electronic medium, will differ from a similar piece of instruction that is presented on the pages of a conventional textbook. Some of these differences are obvious. On a computer screen, images of letters or objects are etched phosphorescently on an electronic medium. In a book, they are inked on a page. On a computer screen, instruction requires electric power and electronic circuitry. On the pages of a book, instruction needs no such equipment.

In some ways, computer screens, because they can be programmed to take advantage of *time,* provide a more flexible instructional medium. For example, computer screens can make text appear and disappear bit by bit, highlight phrases for a specified amount of time, flash certain words on and off to attract attention, or erase and rewrite material when directed to do so by an author or programmer. Books cannot take advantage of timed displays in this same way.

Instruction presented on a computer screen, however, also has a number of disadvantages when compared to instruction presented in a book. The material appearing on a series of computer screens, in the broadest sense, is linear—one screen must follow another, one screen must be erased before another appears. As a result, scanning and skimming may be more difficult on a series of screens than in a book. Some users think that advancing a computer display using a keyboard is more distracting than simply turning a page. Display quality may also cause problems. Screen resolution on certain computers does not always permit the clearest presentation of text and graphics, and some users may find screen displays hard to read for this reason. Finally, the computer is still considered by some individuals to be a nontraditional print medium, and, as such, it may inspire less than total confidence. Fortunately, our students are being exposed to computers at increasingly early ages and are becoming more comfortable with computer use.

In working to refine successive drafts of a CAI lesson, authors should think about how the unique medium of the computer screen will affect instruction. Authors must learn, for instance, how to be consistent in using the various areas of a computer screen (called, hereafter, *functional areas*) to ensure consistency from screen to screen throughout a lesson.[1] Without systematic attention to the location of instructional information on a computer screen, a CAI lesson can be hopelessly confusing and frustrating for students to use. In addition, authors must decide how, and to what extent, to use the special effects available on a computer in presenting instructional materials.

In this chapter, we discuss two broad areas of concern in connection with designing screens for CAI lessons.

1. How can an author identify those functional areas that are needed in a CAI lesson, plan and arrange these areas, and use functional areas in revising a screen-by-screen lesson script?

2. How can an author recognize and identify special effects, plan these effects, and determine which effects will enhance instruction?

Identifying Functional Areas

Most CAI lessons set apart consistent areas or locations on computer screens for certain types of material. These areas, called functional areas, are used to promote consistency and keep students from becoming disoriented as they move from screen to screen throughout a lesson. Organizing instructional material in consistent functional areas allows students to orient themselves quickly to each screen and, as a result, facilitates concentration on learning tasks. An example can help explain the concept of functional areas. In figure 6.1 we show two screens that follow one another in sequence, but do not take advantage of consistent functional areas.

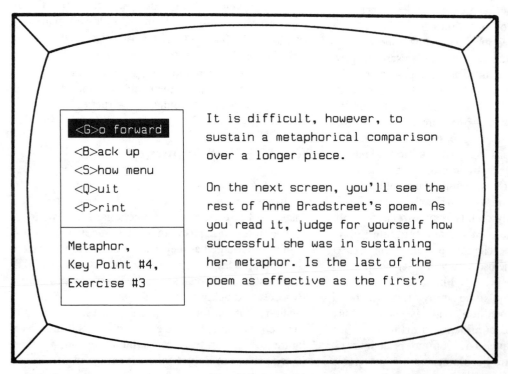

Figure 6.1: Two-Screen Series Which Does Not Use Consistent Functional Areas

The first (or top screen) in this sequence sets up some expectations for the next screen: users expect to find that certain types of material (teaching information, directions, prompts for student response) appear in the same general location on the next screen (bottom screen). Because the information on the second screen does not appear in the same location, users will experience momentary confusion. The same confusion would confront readers of books if the text on one page ran horizontally while the text on the next page ran vertically.

For a contrast, look at the same sequence of screens in figure 6.2. This time we have designed both screens so that they employ consistent functional areas.

If you are like most readers, you found the latter sequence easier to read than the former, because it employs a consistent use of functional areas.

The type of screen an author is designing (instructional screen, help screen, response screen, etc.), will have quite a bit to do with the functional areas to be included. Below, we have identified the most common kinds of functional areas seen in CAI. Read the descriptions, and keep your own script in mind.

Instruction

The great majority of screens in a CAI lesson will be teaching or instructional screens. On these screens, and for some other types of screens (help screens or introductory screens, for example) most authors will want to set apart a fairly large area for text and graphic displays that teach. As figure 6.3 indicates, this instructional area can shrink or expand according to the amount of material that must be presented. However, the area itself should be consistently located.

Because the instructional area is so important in most CAI lessons, it is probably best located near the center of the screen. In Figure 6.4, for instance, the functional area containing instruction must share the center of the screen with the functional areas containing orientation information and screen prompts. Thus, all three areas compete for the viewer's attention. As figure 6.5 shows, the central area of a screen can also be used for giving feedback on student input, another form of instruction.

Directions

Especially on screens that require students to type in responses, most authors designate a special, centrally located area for directions, as in figure 6.6. Generally, although not always, this area should be close to the area in which students type their responses. Again, a consistent location is the key; students should always know where to look for directions.

Student Responses

CAI destined for a writing-intensive classroom (especially one that emphasizes a process-oriented rather than a product-oriented approach) must be designed to accommodate longer responses from students than most other types of CAI. For this reason, it is often important, especially on response screens, to set aside a generous area for student input. On the screen depicted in figure 6.7, for instance, the relatively large functional area for student responses is highlighted and boxed.

The area for student responses should also incorporate a standard symbol (such as ">", "?", or "*") that indicates where the user should start typing material. Often this symbol flashes to rivet students' attention on the response area. To allow this area to accommodate longer responses from students, scrolling can be used so that input moves or "scrolls" up within the boundaries of the response area—all other areas of the screen remaining fixed. If you choose to use this scrolling technique, it is usually advisable to provide students with options that allow them to scroll up *and* down so that they can review what they have written and add additional text.

Choices and Menus

Almost every screen in a CAI lesson should contain a functional area devoted to choices (also called menus). Main menus in a lesson can be used to give students large-scale choices in material or individualized paths through the instruction. Local menus can be used to provide a choice of options in a particular writing exercise or in a multiple choice question. Most authors want each screen of their CAI lesson to offer students some standard choices: move forward one screen; back up one screen; quit the program; see help, menu, or orientation screens; get their writing printed on paper; or send their writing to a computer file. Often these standard choices are displayed in one line at the bottom or top of each lesson screen. On the screen depicted in figure 6.8, for instance, the functional area devoted to choices or menus is highlighted and located at the bottom of the screen. These choice lines, because they afford student users some measure of control over their instruction, are one method of humanizing computer-assisted instruction.

```
Metaphor, Key Point #3, Exercise #3
─────────────────────────────────────────────────

Sometimes poets use metaphor
to dramatize a point. Look at
the following excerpt from the
beginning of Anne Bradstreet's
"The Author To Her Book."

Thou ill-formed offspring of my feeble brain,
Who after birth did'st by my side remain,
Till snatched from thence by friends, less wise than true,
Who thee abroad exposed to public view...

<G>o forward, <B>ack up, <S>how menu, <Q>uit, <P>rint
```

```
Metaphor, Key Point #4, Exercise #3
─────────────────────────────────────────────────

It is difficult, however, to sustain a metaphorical
comparison over a longer piece.

On the next screen, you'll see the rest of Anne
Bradstreet's poem. As you read it, judge for
yourself how successful she was in sustaining
her metaphor. Is the last of the poem as effec-
tive as the first?

<G>o forward, <B>ack up, <S>how menu, <Q>uit, <P>rint
```

Figure 6.2: Two-Screen Series Which Does Use Consistent Functional Areas

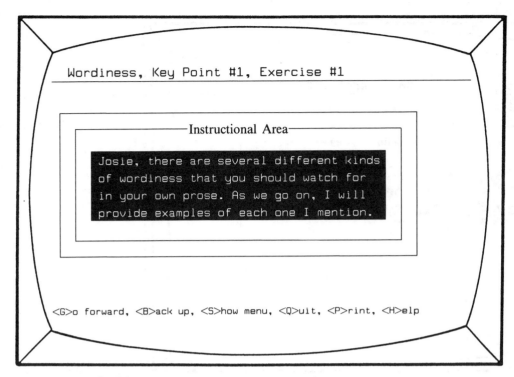

Figure 6.3: Instructional Area

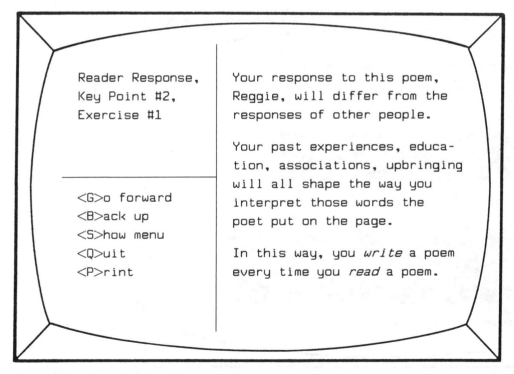

Figure 6.4: Non-Central Location of Instructional Area

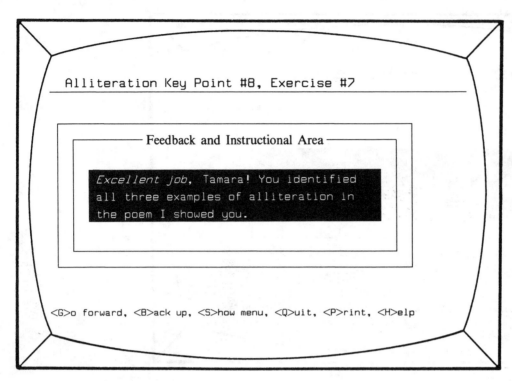

Figure 6.5: Feedback in Instructional Area

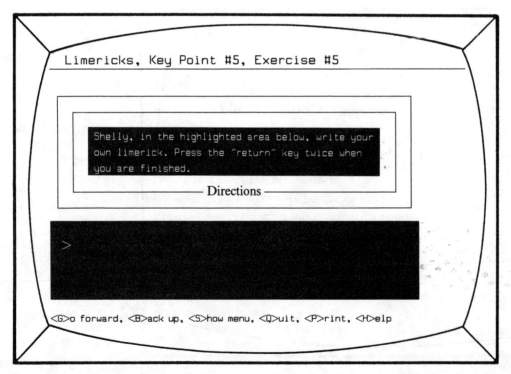

Figure 6.6: Functional Area for Directions

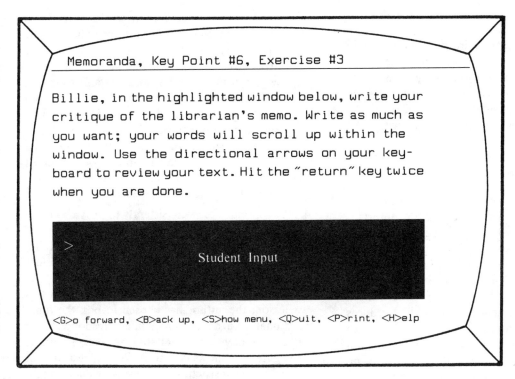

Figure 6.7: Functional Area for Student Input

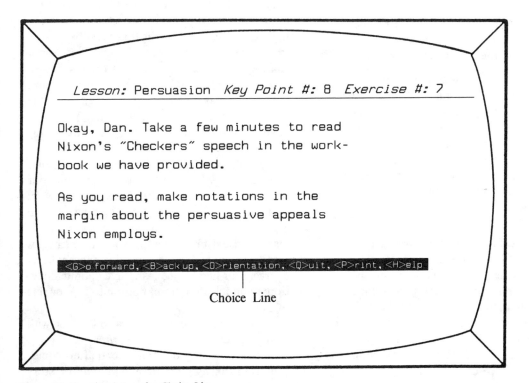

Figure 6.8: Functional Area for Choice Line

Error Messages

Especially on screens that require students to type in some sort of response, authors will want to designate a specific area in which error messages (messages telling students that their input is problematic in some way) appear. Figure 6.9 shows a screen in which the functional area for error messages is nested within the functional area for student responses.

Orientation Information

Some experts suggest devoting one line of each screen in a CAI lesson to orientation information—information that tells students what lesson they are working on and where in that lesson they are currently located. In figure 6.10, the functional area for orientation information is located in a highlighted bar across the top of the screen. An alternative to setting aside a functional space for an orientation line (which reduces the size of functional areas that can be devoted to instruction or student responses) is providing an "orientation" choice in the standard choice, or menu, line. Students can then choose to access orientation information when they feel the need to do so.

Planning Functional Areas

There are a few important guidelines to remember about functional areas when designing screens for CAI lessons. We have outlined them in the following list.

1. Identify the various types of screens your CAI lesson now uses (instructional, introductory, exercise-testing, orientation, etc.). For each kind of screen you identify, list the functional areas that will be required, and then design a screen prototype. This prototype can then be used as a template for designing all other screens of this type. In figure 6.11, we have included sample screen prototypes for an instructional screen, an exercise-testing screen, and a menu screen.

2. Be consistent in locating functional areas. Even though you might have different templates for exercise-testing screens, instructional screens, and help screens, reserve the same general locations for the functional areas they have in common. For example, always place choice, or menu, lines on the last line of a screen, whether that screen is used for displaying instruction, exercise-testing, or introductory material.

3. A rectangle or square is the easiest functional area with which to work, both for you and your programmer. You can make rectangles long and narrow (see the prompt line at the bottom of the screen in figure 6.8) or short and wide (see the instructional area in figure 6.3), but avoid letting one functional area intrude into the space devoted to another functional area. In figure 6.12, for instance, the functional area reserved for choice prompts at the bottom of the screen cuts into the functional area reserved for instruction in the center of the screen.

4. Use special effects consistently to provide visible borders for functional areas. For example, always use the same border to designate the functional area devoted to student responses. Figure 6.7, for instance, represents a frame from a CAI lesson on writing effective memoranda. In this lesson, the author has chosen to box the functional area devoted to student responses as a consistent visual cue for student users. Similarly, figure 6.8 shows a screen from a lesson that makes a consistent use of reverse video to highlight the functional area devoted to the standard choice, or menu, line.

5. Experiment with using various methods of clearing and filling entire screens and individual functional areas. An author can choose to erase individual functional areas that must be cleared from the screen, leaving intact those that do not change from frame to frame. In the two-screen sequence represented by figure 6.13, for instance, the author has cleared and replaced only the top half of the screen (the functional area devoted to directions), leaving the bottom portion of the screen (the functional areas devoted to students' responses and to the standard choice line) unchanged. Ask the programmer on your team to demonstrate the difference between clearing a screen or functional area with a *pop* erase (images disappear at once, creating a distinct visual break) and a *wipe* erase (images disappear more slowly—usually character by character or line by line—and in a definite direction: from top to bottom, bottom to top, or side to side).

   Filling screens or areas can also be done with different techniques such as *time delays* (an answer is displayed one full second after a question is displayed) or *directional fills* (a story

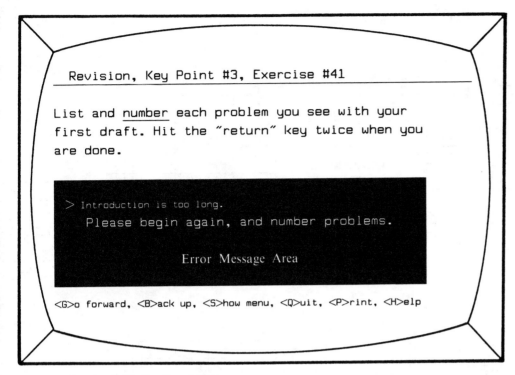

Figure 6.9: Functional Area For Error Messages

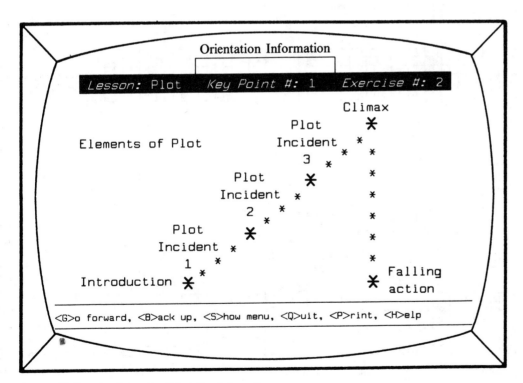

Figure 6.10: Functional Area for Orientation Information

Prototypes for Screens

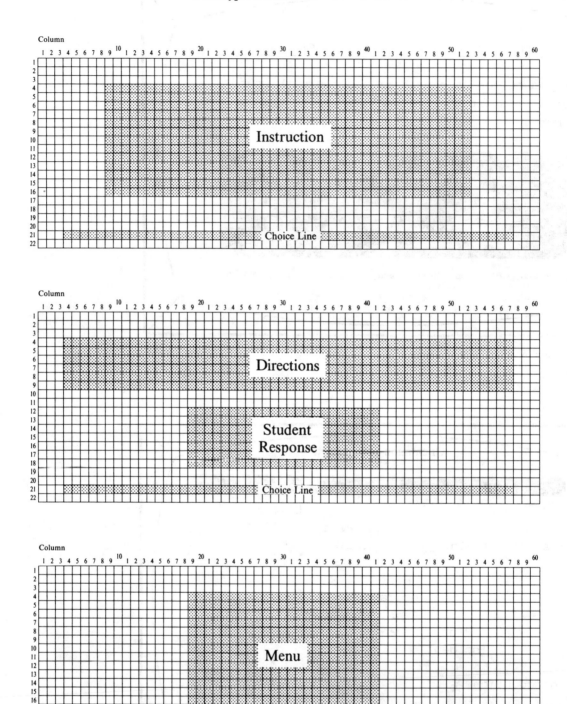

Figure 6.11: Prototypes for Instructional, Exercise-Testing, and Menu Screens

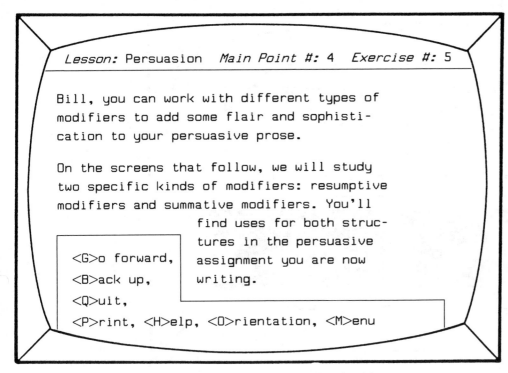

Lesson: Persuasion   *Main Point #:* 4   *Exercise #:* 5

Bill, you can work with different types of
modifiers to add some flair and sophistication to your persuasive prose.

On the screens that follow, we will study
two specific kinds of modifiers: resumptive
modifiers and summative modifiers. You'll
find uses for both struc-
tures in the persuasive
<G>o forward,   assignment you are now
<B>ack up,   writing.
<Q>uit,
<P>rint, <H>elp, <O>rientation, <M>enu

Figure 6.12: L-Shaped Functional Area That Intrudes into Another Functional Area

displayed line by line and from top to bottom to increase suspense).

6. Whenever possible, let students control the lesson environment, especially the rate at which screens are displayed, the direction in which screens move, and the duration of a lesson. When dealing with computers, human beings should feel as if they are in control, as if they have power over the technology they are using. Teachers and CAI authors can empower their students at the most basic level by providing "move forward," "move backward," and "quit" options in the prompt line for each screen.

After reading the information we have just provided on screen design and functional areas, you may want to review your own CAI script and come up with some new screen designs. The first step in such a review involves identifying the functional areas that you need for each type of screen used in your lesson. In figure 6.14, we show how Jean might have accomplished such a review using a worksheet to keep track of her thinking.

As figure 6 .14 indicates, Jean completed the review task for two types of screens in her script: menu screens and instructional screens. She identified two functional areas that she needed to include on her menu screens (a *choice* area and a *directions* area), and three functional areas she needed to include on her instruction screens (an area for *instruction,* an area for *orientation information,* and an area for *choices and menus*). Later, Jean would complete a similar activity for the other types of screens she includes in her CAI script.

The second step we suggest for reviewing screen designs in your lesson involves creating templates. Figure 6.15 shows a template that Jean might have created for the menu screens in her freewriting lesson.

Jean's template for menu screens, you may have noted, provides a location for the two functional areas she identified in the last activity: an area for choices or menus, and an area for directions. This frame protocol, or template, will make a useful tool for a team programmer. Because it has been constructed on a sheet that identifies columns and rows, the programmer will know exactly where on each screen to locate text from the script.

At the end of this chapter, we provide two worksheets to help you with your own screen-design efforts: Worksheet 21: Planning Functional Areas for a CAI Lesson and Worksheet 22: Designing Screen Displays. On these worksheets, you are invited to identify functional areas for each type of screen in your lesson and create screen templates for use in revising your screen-

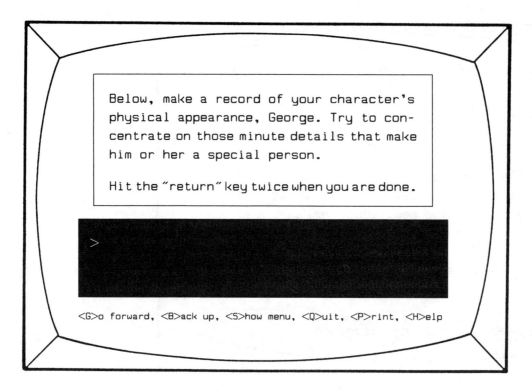

Figure 6.13: Two-Screen Series That Clears a Single Functional Area

Example of Planning Functional Areas for a CAI Lesson

Screen Type 1:

Menu Screens

Functional Areas Needed:

an area for the menu choices themselves
an area for menu directions

Notes:

Only small area needed for directions—use almost the same directions each time.

Screen Type 2:

Instructional Screens

Functional Areas Needed:

an area for the instruction itself
an area for orientation information
an area for menu choices

Notes:

Check with programmer to verify screen dimensions—preserve 20-character margins on each side.
Orientation information should go at top of screen, choices at the bottom.

Figure 6.14: Sample of Worksheet 20 Activity

by-screen lesson script. You can turn to these worksheets now and complete the activities or finish reading the rest of this chapter first.

Identifying Special Effects in a CAI Lesson

The use of the computer screen as a medium for instruction allows authors to take advantage of certain presentation techniques that are usually eye-catching. Often referred to as special effects, these techniques may include the use of color, special typefaces, sound, animation, or time delays. Among other things, these effects make it possible to enhance the presentation of instructional material, focus students' attention on one segment of the screen, or identify the placement of student input. In the list that follows, we have identified the various kinds of special effects that authors of CAI can employ. Read this list, keeping in mind the project you are planning.

Timing

Dynamic special effects can be created by using the computer's ability to tell time. Authors can, with the help of a programmer, design screens so that they appear line by line or sentence by sentence at designated intervals. This effect, for example, can be used to advantage in cloze-type reading activities that ask students to predict the information that will appear next. Authors can also design time-delay screens that display a question and wait a predetermined time before displaying an answer, underlining a request, or flashing a prompt for student input.

Color

Some computers have the ability to display information in different colors. Color can be used to highlight letters, sentences, or paragraphs; to mark areas in which students type responses; or to emphasize particularly important directions. To take advantage of this special effect, a computer must have a color monitor. Ask your team's programmer for information about the color capabilities of the computer you plan to use for your lesson.

Recall

Screens can be designed so that they display material that students typed earlier in the lesson. The screen in figure 6.16 shows how such a recall feature can work. In a review activity located at the end of a session, the computer recalls and displays a list of main points students identified in an earlier reading comprehension activity. Such special effects are especially useful in a process-based writing classroom because they are amenable to activities that require recursive attention to material.

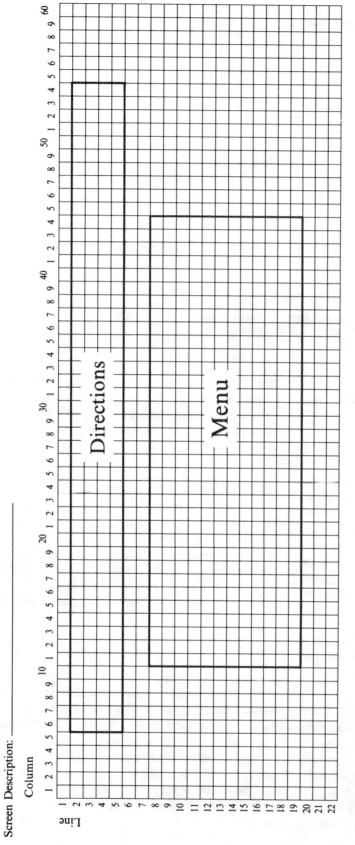

Figure 6.15: Sample Template for Menu Screens

Animation

CAI lessons can animate all sorts of things. Authors can make sentences, words, and paragraphs move from one location to another; display a plot line that extends itself with each additional narrative event; or show a revision in the making. Again, the sophistication of the animation your computer can handle may be limited. Check with the team programmer for details.

Underlining, Flashing, Reverse Video

CAI lessons can employ underlining (regular or time-delayed), flashing (blinking items), and reverse video (highlighting) to call students' attention to single letters, clusters of words, paragraphs, sentences, nouns, passive constructions, or anything else you might want. In figure 6.17, for example, the author calls students' attention to a passive construction in a response by highlighting the sentence element on the screen. Flashing can alternate between two colors, regular and reverse-video, or on and off.

Graphics

Authors can design screens in a CAI lesson to take advantage of a wide range of graphic elements: boxes, lines, arrows, pictures, borders, bars, concrete poetry, etc. The team programmer can identify the graphics displays that can be produced on the computer for which your lesson is designed.

Scrolling

A computer screen can display only a limited amount of material at one time. However, material can be scrolled (moved onto the screen) vertically or horizontally. This technique is especially helpful in managing lengthy passages that students write. A long piece of prose or poetry can be scrolled automatically or at the command of the user.

Typefaces and Sizes

Some computers allow authors to select (or design) and use different typefaces on a CAI lesson screen; bold, Elizabethan English, sans serif, italic, and shadowed faces are common. On some computers, authors can also adjust the size of fonts.

Sound

Some lessons that authors design may benefit from the addition of sound. For example, a teacher might want to have the computer beep or buzz after students have written for five or ten minutes, or sound an alarm when classes are about to change. Some computers can generate and reproduce human speech, although this effect is not commonly found on equipment purchased for student use.

Add-Ons

Special effects can also be obtained through the use of light pens (penlike attachments that allow students to mark, draw, or write directly on the screen), graphics tablets (small pads on which students can draw images which appear on the computer screen), or movement devices (joy sticks, roller balls, or dials that allow users to direct screen images with hand controls). Keep in mind that these add-ons can be expensive and are not common on most computers purchased for student use.

Planning Special Effects for a CAI Lesson

There are a few important guidelines to remember about special effects when designing screens for a CAI lesson. We have outlined them in the following list of suggestions.

1. Consult with experts. Not all computers can provide the same special effects. The technical people who maintain the computers or the team programmer should be consulted *before* an author begins designing special effects into the screen presentations of a CAI lesson.

2. Keep it simple! Used inappropriately, whistles, bells, or flashing colors may distract, rather than focus, users. Consider the purpose of the instruction, the age of the students, and the number of times a lesson will be used when planning special effects.

3. Review successful CAI. Choose those programs you like the most and take notes on which special effects are employed, when these effects are used, and how they are used. Then try adapting some of the same techniques to your own CAI.

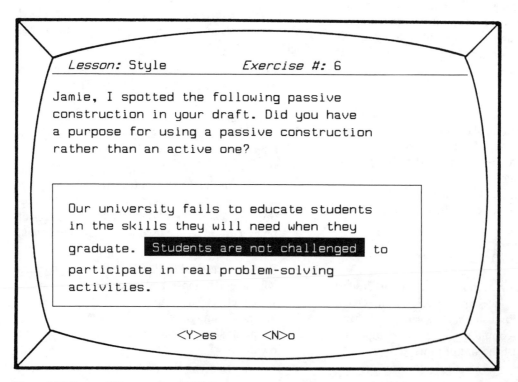

```
┌─────────────────────────────────────────────────┐
│  Lesson: Improving Comprehension Exercise #: Final Exam
│                                                   │
│  Ann, here are the three main comprehension       │
│  points you identified when you first started     │
│  this lesson.                                      │
│                                                   │
│     ┌───────────────────────────────────────┐    │
│     │   1. Computers can't "read" like us.   │    │
│     │   2. Engineers are working to develop  │    │
│     │        artificial intelligence in computers │
│     │        that resembles our own intelligence. │
│     │   3. "Human" language is the main barrier in │
│     │        this effort.                    │    │
│     └───────────────────────────────────────┘    │
│                                                   │
│  <G>o forward, <B>ack up, <S>how menu, <Q>uit, <P>rint, <H>elp
└─────────────────────────────────────────────────┘
```

Figure 6.16: Recall as a Special Effect

```
┌─────────────────────────────────────────────────┐
│    Lesson: Style              Exercise #: 6       │
│                                                   │
│  Jamie, I spotted the following passive           │
│  construction in your draft. Did you have         │
│  a purpose for using a passive construction       │
│  rather than an active one?                        │
│                                                   │
│     ┌───────────────────────────────────────┐    │
│     │  Our university fails to educate students │  │
│     │  in the skills they will need when they │    │
│     │  graduate. [Students are not challenged] to │ │
│     │  participate in real problem-solving   │    │
│     │  activities.                            │    │
│     └───────────────────────────────────────┘    │
│                                                   │
│              <Y>es       <N>o                     │
└─────────────────────────────────────────────────┘
```

Figure 6.17: Reverse Video as a Special Effect

4. Field test special effects. When there is a question about whether a particular special effect works, arrange to have a small sample of your target audience try it out or test the effect on a sample of colleagues who come in contact with this target audience. In the written surveys used as part of a field-testing effort, ask specific questions about whether a special effect distracts from or enhances your lesson.

5. Think about transfer. If you plan to have other teachers in a department, school, or district use a CAI lesson, limit special effects to those that are commonly found on most available computers. Including more sophisticated effects, such as color displays, for instance, may limit the kinds of computers to which a CAI lesson will be transferable. Talk to the programmer and to the marketing expert on your team about which computers handle the special effects you desire and which computers are the most popular with the target audience you have identified. Then, choose special effects accordingly.

6. Be precise about identifying special effects on screen-by-screen lesson scripts. As you go back to revise the screen-by-screen script for your CAI lesson, be sure to make systematic notations about the special effects you want on each screen. The more information you can provide the team's programmer about the effects you want to achieve, the easier his or her job will be.

After reading this section on special effects, you might want to review your own CAI script to evaluate how well such effects have been employed in the lesson you are planning. We think it is worth your while to locate each screen that requires special effects, document these effects thoroughly for the team programmer, and systematically check your original decisions. Figure 6.18 shows how Jean might have undertaken such a review for one screen within her freewriting lesson. Jean's observations and notes are recorded on a special worksheet designed for this purpose.

As you can see, Jean has planned to use two different special effects on the screen she is reviewing: colored areas and blinking characters. She wants the student response box on the screen to be a light blue in color, and she wants the cursor (the > sign) in this box to blink. Although Jean has thought carefully about the use of both special effects, she has made a note to field test how effective the use of color is with students in her target audience. Making systematic notes, like Jean's, on the use of special effects will not only provide valuable information for the team programmer (who must know exactly *where* each special effect is to be located, *what* it is to look like, and *how long* it is to last) but also important direction for later field-testing efforts.

At the end of this chapter on Worksheet 23: Thinking about Special Effects in a CAI Lesson, we will provide you with similar worksheets to use in reviewing the special effects for your own CAI lesson.

Summary

In this chapter, we discussed why displays on a computer screen can be, at once, both more flexible and more limited than those in a more conventional print medium like a book. We mentioned that, unlike a printed page, the computer screen can take advantage of the dimension of *time* to present information in a predetermined sequence or pace, but that it is essentially a linear medium that requires users to become familiar with the concept of having only one screen visible at any one time.

We also introduced the concept of functional areas as a means for organizing screen displays and suggested reserving different functional areas for instruction, directions, student responses, choice lines, error messages, and orientation information. We suggested that authors make these decisions depending on the type of screen display (teaching screen, exercise-testing screen, help screen, etc.) being planned.

Special effects that could enhance screen displays were also covered briefly. We suggested trying a variety of effects, among them timing, color, recall, animation, underlining, reverse video, flashing, graphics, scrolling, typefaces and sizes, sound, and add-ons. When planning special effects to include in your CAI instruction, do not forget to field test those effects that have the potential of distracting learners.

Note

1. For the term *functional areas* and for many of the concepts I cover in this chapter, I am indebted to Jesse M. Heines and his text *Screen Design Strategies for Computer-Assisted Instruction.* In this chapter, I attempt to adapt and apply Mr. Heines's thinking to the field of composition instruction.

Example of Thinking about Special Effects in a CAI Lesson

Screen: __2.3 Automatic Freewriting Sequence__

Special Effect 1: __color-blue__   Line Numbers: __12–18__

Explanation: __Use to identify location for student responses—entire scrolling, boxed area is blue. Box__

__outlined in darker blue. See Exercise-Screen template for box location.__

Special Effect 2: __blinking__   Line Numbers: __12__

Explanation: __The > prompt that signals students where to begin writing should blink on and off.__

__Locate in column 21, line 12.__

(YES)	NO	Appropriate for the target audience
(YES)	NO	Attracts rather than distracts students
(YES)	NO	Helps accomplish the general purpose of the lesson and the specific goals of the instructional objective
(YES)	NO	Can be done on computers available to target audience
YES	(NO)	Can be transferred to a number of other computers
(YES)	NO	Should be field tested at a later time

Notes: Use a very light blue for the student response areas. I don't want it to distract attention from the directions for the writing task. Field test effectiveness of colored response box with target audience.

Figure 6.18: Sample of Worksheet 22 Activity

Worksheet 20: Planning Functional Areas for a CAI Lesson

To complete this worksheet, you will need the latest draft of your screen-by-screen lesson script and a copy of Worksheet 15: Identifying Possible Screen Types. Make a copy of this form for each screen type you identified on Worksheet 15. Determine the functional areas that will need to be reserved for each screen type and identify them as either instructions, directions, student responses, choice prompts, orientation information, or error messages.

Screen Type ⎯⎯⎯⎯⎯⎯⎯⎯⎯⎯⎯⎯⎯⎯⎯⎯⎯⎯⎯⎯⎯⎯⎯⎯⎯⎯⎯⎯⎯⎯⎯⎯⎯

Functional Areas Needed:

118   *Cynthia L. Selfe*

Worksheet 21: Designing Screen Displays for a CAI Lesson

Using the notes you have made on Worksheet 20: Planning Functional Areas for a CAI Lesson, use copies of this grid to design a general prototype for each screen type you have identified.

Screen Description: _____

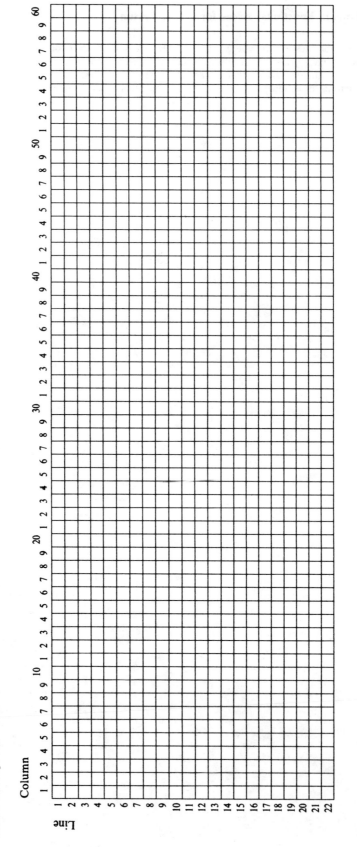

Notes:

Worksheet 22: Thinking about Special Effects in a CAI Lesson

To complete this worksheet, you will need the latest draft of the screen-by-screen script for you CAI lesson. For each screen of your script that requires a special effect, make a copy of this form.

After identifying the special effects to include on each screen in your CAI lesson, use the guidelines that follow to double-check your decisions for each screen.

Special Effect 1: _____   Line Numbers: _____

Explanation: _____

Special Effect 2: _____   Line Numbers: _____

Explanation: _____

Special Effect 3: _____   Line Numbers: _____

Explanation: _____

YES   NO   Appropriate for the target audience

YES   NO   Attracts rather than distracts students

YES   NO   Helps accomplish the general purpose of the lesson and the specific goals of
                         the instructional objective

YES   NO   Can be done on computers available to target audience

YES   NO   Can be transferred to a number of other computers

YES   NO   Should be field tested at a later time

Notes:

Worksheet 22 continued

7 FIELD TESTING A CAI LESSON

When you have revised the screen-by-screen script of your lesson several times and have a programmed version of the instruction running on a computer, your team is ready to begin a systematic program of field testing. No matter how hard an author works to write and revise a CAI lesson and a team works to refine content, presentation, and pedagogy, many problems will remain undetected until the lesson is field tested in realistic situations. Unfortunately, the time allotted to field testing is often minimal. Teachers and authors want to get their lesson up and running in the classroom, marketing managers want to sell their product to software houses, and distributors want to get their product to consumers.

In the team-oriented process described in this book, however, field testing figures centrally. It provides the impetus for quality control and the directed revision of your lesson. We urge you to *make* time for field testing for several reasons. First, a thorough field-testing effort will help you safeguard your own reputation—after all, your CAI lesson has your name on it, and any problems it may have will reflect on you. Second, field testing will ensure high quality instruction for those students who use your lesson. Finally, field testing will contribute, in a general and important sense, to higher standards for CAI produced in the discipline of writing instruction.

This chapter will answer some of the major questions authors have about field testing.

1. What lesson components should be field tested?
2. When should field testing take place?
3. How should field testing be undertaken?
4. Who should be involved in field testing?

The worksheets at the end of the chapter will help your team design its field-testing effort.

What Lesson Components Should Be Field Tested?

In the final analysis, it will be up to the composition specialist—the director of the design team—to deter-mine how extensive the field-testing effort will be. Other team members, of course, will have suggestions, but this specialist may need to serve as the main quality-control officer. Fortunately, *any* field testing that the team undertakes will be useful; however, the more time put into testing and refining a CAI lesson, the better it will become as a piece of instruction.

Although each lesson demands a different program of field testing, there are some basic lesson components around which your team will want to design specific field-testing questions, investigations, and situations.

Instructional Objectives

The field-testing program for every CAI lesson should include, at some point, a systematic evaluation of instructional objectives. This evaluation will help a design team determine whether students can accomplish the instructional objectives identified as part of the CAI lesson (Worksheet 14). If the team has followed the process outlined in this book, such an evaluation will be relatively straightforward: each instructional objective identified for the lesson will have evaluation criteria attached to it. (See pages 47–48 for a review of instructional objectives.)

To plan this component of a field-testing program, first update and revise the list of instructional objectives you compiled earlier. Make sure that it reflects revisions in the final screen-by-screen lesson script of your lesson or revisions made in adapting the lesson for programming purposes. Next, arrange for a sample of students to use the lesson. Recording users' performance on each instructional objective will give your team an accurate picture of where the lesson succeeds or fails in the task of teaching. This kind of systematic testing of each instructional objective will also help you pinpoint where revision of the lesson is needed.

Lesson Attractiveness

Most teams will also want to find out how students *like* the CAI lesson when they use it. No matter how effective the lesson is in getting students to accomplish instructional objectives, it must also be attractive to them. Part of most field-testing efforts should be devoted to finding out how students rate the lesson's interest level, tone, persona, examples, and activities. Your team might, for instance, want to ask whether students perceive themselves as being challenged by the instruction; whether they think the writing exercises boring, too lengthy, or less than creative; or whether they would recommend the program to their friends.

Ease of Use

Field testing is also valuable in identifying ease-of-use problems, those problems stemming from the structural features of the lesson. For example, a team may want to determine whether students can access the lesson by themselves, use menus and help screens to work their way through the instruction, or understand directions in individual activities. Testing for ease of use might also involve checking the readability levels of screen text or the hard-copy documentation that accompanies a lesson, recording the time that it takes students to learn to use the commands associated with a lesson, or cataloging the questions students ask when using a lesson.

Classroom Fit

Field testing can also identify how teachers and students see a CAI lesson fitting into regular classroom routine or activities. When field testing a CAI lesson, a design team may want to ask teachers and students *when* they think the lesson could be used most profitably (inside or outside the classroom, at the beginning or end of a term, during prewriting or revising efforts), *where* the lesson should be housed (writing lab, classroom, learning center), and *who* would find the lesson most useful.

Content

If there is only one composition expert working on a CAI team and monitoring the content of a lesson, the team may want to submit the content of the unit to a reading by other writing specialists. Other scholars with expertise in the teaching of composition or rhetoric can provide fresh perspectives on the instruction's content, the rhetorical theory (or theories) upon which it is based, and the pedagogy it represents.

Biases

Bias, in both the language and content in a CAI lesson, can affect learners' success. A field-testing program can investigate whether the language or the examples in a CAI lesson are more accessible to certain cultural, ethnic, or gender groups than others. For example, the use of gender-biased language or examples may prove to offend teachers as well as students and may thus limit the usefulness of a CAI lesson with certain groups.

Surface Features

Field testing can also help design teams catch grammar, usage, and spelling mistakes. Some of these mistakes escape detection in the screen-by-screen lesson script and are transferred verbatim into the lesson's program; others are introduced by the programmer in the process of coding the lesson or by a secretary involved in typing some part of the lesson. In any case, most field-testing trials serve a valuable proofreading function.

After reading over these suggestions for field testing, you might want to think about identifying a field-testing program for your own CAI lesson. We suggest a four-step process for this project. As a first step toward this goal, you will want to review the screen-by-screen script of your lesson, looking especially for activities that are confusing, overly difficult, boring, or inappropriate for a target audience. Make a list of the instructional objectives connected with these activities. Second, look for parts of the lesson that are unattractive or hard to use. List these lesson components for later reference. Third, list those questions you have about how the lesson will fit into your writing program or classroom. Finally, identify any reservations or questions you might have about the lesson's content or biases. All of these activities will provide information that you can use later in designing a field-testing program to fit your lesson. The following list shows how Jean might have completed such a field-testing review for her lesson on freewriting.

Example of Identifying Field-Testing Questions

1. List the instructional objectives that would benefit from field testing. Choose activities that are confusing, overly difficult, boring, inappropriate, or unfinished.

   I am not happy about part of the "Keeping a Journal" activity. My central objective is to get students to keep a journal on the computer for a week—making at least five entries and writing for at least twenty minutes each entry. Are journal writes best done on a computer or in the privacy of a dorm room? Will students feel constrained about writing very private, risky expressive discourse on the computers in a writing lab? Test this.

2. List questions about the lesson's attractiveness. Consider such things as tone, the computer persona used in the instruction, screen-design techniques, examples, writing activities, organization, length, etc.

   Test the following three components: 1. persona (too cute?), 2. journal examples (too long? distracting?), and 3. lesson length (too long for one sitting?).

3. List those questions you have about the lesson's ease of use.

   Test these questions: Can a student in my class follow the directions I've provided for turning on the computer and accessing the lesson? Is the initial menu confusing? Are there additional places where "help" screens are needed? Is the screen text at an appropriate reading level?

4. List questions about how the lesson will fit into a writing classroom or program.

   Check to see if the lesson could be used by a student, without a tutor's aid, in our writing lab.

5. List reservations about the lesson's content.

   Should the lesson include a discussion of diaries? Does the discussion of freewriting as a strategy represent the most current information the profession has about writing, the writing process, and writing theory?

6. List questions about the biases reflected in this lesson and their impact on an audience. Consider cultural, economic, language, and gender biases among others.

   None that I can see right now.

At the end of this chapter, we have included a form (Worksheet 22: Identifying Field-Testing Questions) that will help you think about the field testing needed for your own CAI lesson. You can turn to this worksheet now and complete the tasks it describes or finish reading the rest of this chapter first.

When Should Field Testing Take Place?

Some authors like to wait until they have a fairly "clean" version of a CAI lesson up and running on a computer before they begin field-testing efforts. However, there are some very good arguments for integrating field testing into the early stages of a CAI project.

First, the process of writing CAI is like that of writing any other technical material destined for a specific target audience—the more feedback you get and the earlier you get it, the easier the later stages of the project can be. In the early stages of writing CAI, you might have only the barest outline of a lesson, some lists of activities you want to put on the computer, or a very rough draft of a script. However, a colleague, at your own institution or somewhere else, might be able to give these materials a quick reading (an early, informal field test) and provide a fresh theoretical perspective on the lesson, suggest additional writing activities, or even refer you to similar CAI already on the market.

Second, getting early feedback on your lesson may save money in the long run. As a project develops, it becomes more of a team effort and, as a result, more costly to change. If, for example, you decide late in the development process that a certain writing activity has to be modified, you are prescribing additional work not only for yourself as the author who must compose a new segment of the script, but also for the programmer, who must write new code, and for the educational specialist, who must work with new instructional objectives and evaluation techniques for that activity. Beginning field-testing efforts *early* in the design process—asking colleagues to read and respond to drafts of a screen-by-screen script, getting students to try out each writing activity as it is developed by the design team—will help you avoid larger and more costly changes at a later point in the process.

We suggest thinking of field testing as a process parallel to that of writing and developing CAI. Thus, field testing should be taking place all the time. In the early stages of developing a lesson, authors can share plans, outlines, or drafts of the script informally with colleagues. As the lesson develops, try ideas, format presentations, or individual instructional activities on students in classes, other faculty who teach composition, or team members. If you have a problem with a particular section of a lesson, get three students to try it out and see how they perform. If you wonder what

124   *Cynthia L. Selfe*

kind of writing activity would be most effective for the lesson's target audience, ask a few students to choose among three screens featuring alternative choices. During the later stages of development, plan a formal and systematic field-testing effort. Whenever you field test, keep careful records of the results so that you can use the data to shape later versions of the lesson.

After reading about the process of field testing CAI, you may want to design a schedule for testing your own lesson—building in field tests at early stages of the development process as well as a systematic final series of field tests. In figure 7.1, we show how Jean, working on a specially designed scheduling sheet, might have scheduled the field testing for her lesson on freewriting.

As you can see, Jean's field-testing efforts parallel her team's development process. In fact, she plans to field test certain components of her lesson as soon as she completes the second draft of her screen-by-screen script. At the end of this chapter, we have provided a worksheet (Worksheet 24: Scheduling Field Testing) on which you can plan a field-testing schedule for your own CAI lesson. You can turn to this worksheet now or finish reading the rest of this chapter first.

How Should Field Testing Be Undertaken?

Field testing a CAI lesson is an art with which the composition specialist on a design team must become familiar. Most teams will look to the composition specialist as project director and primary author, to decide which components of the lesson must be tested and then to design a method of testing them. If you find yourself in the role of field-testing manager, be creative in designing testing situations; don't limit your approach to one method or idea.

Traditionally, field testing takes place in a laboratory or classroom setting. Students come in, sit down, and run through the entire lesson from start to finish while an observer takes note of any problems they have. The notes are then handed to the author, and a second (and often final) draft of the lesson is produced. Such a narrow approach to field testing, however, provides revision information limited in both scope and accuracy.

Instead of this one-shot, test-everything-at-once strategy, we suggest the following alternatives.

1. Break up initial field-testing efforts so that they focus on only one or two lesson components at

Example of Scheduling a Field-Testing Program

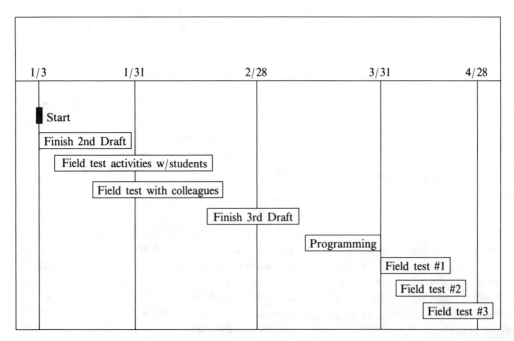

Figure 7.1: Sample of Worksheet 24 Activity

a time. Authors might, for instance, want to focus each test on one or two central issues: for example, testing students' success on the instructional objectives associated with a lesson or checking the lesson's ease of use. This strategy allows a team to identify more accurately *where* and *how* students are having trouble with a lesson and saves time and effort by allowing the design team to concentrate on one component of the lesson at a time.

2. Try a "multiple-offense approach" that employs several different field-testing methods to identify potential rough spots. In the remainder of this section, we have identified a number of field-testing methods: surveys, questionnaires, interviews, pretests and posttests, among others. Encourage your team to combine these methods in their field-testing efforts.

   Consult this list when your team has identified the field-testing program they would like to undertake. For each field test, choose the methods best suited to providing data on the specific lesson components you want to examine. In one field-testing situation, for example, you might want to concentrate on identifying places where the lesson's ease-of-use mechanisms (menus, directions, documentation, commands) break down, causing students to "get stuck." Consult the list of field-testing methods to find out which strategy would provide the most effective way of testing for such information.

   Several techniques might be appropriate in such a situation. You might, for example, ask student users to "think aloud" during a field test and audiotape their stream-of-consciousness responses. You could also videotape students as they use a particular segment of the lesson or query them about specific ease-of-use problems in a questionnaire. You could even instruct students to hit a certain key on the keyboard whenever they become confused, a key that would record where in the lesson the confusion was experienced and present this data in a file designated for your team's later use. Whatever technique or combination of techniques you decide to use, make sure it is appropriate for investigating the lesson component on which you are concentrating.

3. Be as realistic as possible about field testing. Test lesson components on students and teachers similar to those in your target audience. If the material is designed for a range of users, make sure the groups in your sample mirror those in the target population. Match for experience, age, ability level, grade level, background, and other considerations. Separate the field-testing data gathered from each of these groups so that the design team can ascertain whether the lesson is more or less effective for certain groups.

   Also be as realistic as possible about the setting in which the field testing takes place. If the lesson is to be used in a particular course, a writing lab, or a classroom setting, test it in a similar situation so that you can record the effects of distractions, course content, room layouts, kibitzers, or extraneous noise.

Because every CAI lesson demands a different, individualized program of field testing, the methods you use to gather data will vary widely. There are, however, a few relatively simple methods that can be employed individually and in combination to gather data for a systematic program of field testing. We also encourage you, however, to create home-grown methods and instruments to fit the specific field-testing program you are planning.

Surveys and Questionnaires

These instruments can be used to gather data on any number of topics. On surveys or questionnaires, you can ask student users to rate the interest level of the lesson, evaluate the attractiveness of the lesson's persona, indicate the difficulty of any particular activity, and discuss the specific problems they had when using the lesson. In figure 7.2, we provide a number of survey and questionnaire items that could be suitable for student users. Please note the range and variety of the items we have provided: items based on Likert scales or differential scales, circle-the-answer and check-the-answer formats, fill-in-the-blank or completion questions, and short essay questions. Quite probably, you would not choose to employ all of these different kinds of items on one survey or questionnaire. We have given them to you here to indicate the range and variety of techniques available.

Surveys and questionnaires can also be used to gather information from teachers and administrators. These individuals can be asked to identify possible uses or contexts for the lesson in their particular writing program or classroom, to indicate the appropriateness of the lesson's content for their students, or to suggest content revisions. In figure 7.3, we have listed

Survey for Students

1. Rate this lesson's general interest level on the scale below.

not at all interesting		of medium interest		highly interesting
1	2	3	4	5

|—————————|—————————|—————————|—————————|

2. In this lesson, you were asked to do quite a bit of writing. Please give us your response to the writing by placing an "X" somewhere on the continuum below.

    Writing tasks   Writing tasks
     too easy   too difficult

|——|

3. Below, circle those activities that you enjoyed in this lesson.

      freewriting   nutshelling

      automatic writing   character sketches

      brainstorming/listing   review of lecture points

4. Below, check all the appropriate responses.

    ————— I would recommend this lesson to a classmate.

    ————— I would use it again for another writing assignment.

    ————— The lesson made me feel better about writing in general.

    ————— The lesson made me feel more confident about writing this particular assignment.

5. Fill in the blanks below with an appropriate word or phrase.

    This lesson —————————————————————————.

    In general, writing assignments —————————————————.

    The writing assignments in this lesson —————————————.

6. Which activity in this lesson was your least favorite?

Figure 7.2: Sample Survey and Questionnaire Items for Student Users

Survey for Teachers and Administrators

1. Below, please list the writing-intensive courses in which this lesson could be used.

2. Circle the items below which describe the ways in which you (or your writing program) could use this lesson.

    writing lab   class work

    writing classroom   supplement to textbook

    homework   replacement for textbook

3. Below, please identify any gaps you see in the content of the lesson as it now stands.

4. Which of the characteristics below did you like *least* about this lesson? Please circle all appropriate items.

    its length   persona

    review of lecture points   appropriateness for students

    writing assignments   examples

5. If you could change any one thing in this lesson, what would it be?

Figure 7.3: Sample Survey and Questionnaire Items Appropriate for Teachers and Administrators

a number of survey items that are suitable for teachers and administrators. Again, we have included items that take a variety of forms.

Interviews

Oral interviews with students, teachers, and administrators who field test a CAI lesson can yield information that will prove helpful in revision efforts. Interview questions, which should be written down in a standard form, can be asked at any time during a field-testing program: after a user completes a particular writing task ("What did you like or dislike the most about the last writing activity?"), after a user completes an entire section of the lesson ("What additional invention activities would you like students to do in connection with this lesson on writing memoranda?"), or after a user completes the entire lesson ("Did any part of this lesson seem too simple for your students? Too difficult?").

Think-Aloud Protocols

Users can be asked to "think out loud" as they work through a lesson while a team member records their efforts on videotape or audiotape. When transcribed, the videotapes and audiotapes provide valuable information on how individuals react to the lesson, where they get stuck, where they enjoy themselves, where they have questions, where they need help. Below is an excerpt from a teacher who is field testing a lesson for a colleague.

> Okay this thing should be easy . . . so he says. [presses the "enter" key] Well, that doesn't work obviously. If I can't get it started, the kids certainly can't. [text appears on screen] Oh . . . there it goes, not patient enough, I guess . . . should put some sort of "Wait here" sign on the screen for the kids or they'll be pressing every button in sight.

Pretests and Posttests

Testing what students know *before* they use a lesson (or some component of a lesson) and comparing this with what they know *after* they use the lesson can provide valuable data for a design team's revising efforts. These pretests and posttests can be as specific or as general as you wish. You can, for example, give pretests and posttests for each separate instructional objective within your CAI lesson, or you can give more general pretests and posttests for the lesson as a whole.

If you have followed the process we suggested for identifying instructional objectives, designing these pretests and posttests should prove a relatively simple task. First, identify the instructional objectives that you want to field test. Second, using the evaluation criteria you identified for each instructional objective, test students *before* they are exposed to your CAI instruction. Third, ask students to work through those instructional activities for which you are testing. Fourth, using the same evaluation criteria, test the students *after* they have used your CAI lesson. Finally, compare the two performances and record the results in tabular form. In figure 7.4, you can see an example of such a table as Jean might have constructed it during the field testing of her freewriting lesson.

The results of the pretests and posttests represented on this sample chart indicate that at least one instructional activity in Jean's lesson, focused freewriting, might profit from further revision.

Observation

Simple observation of users as they work through a CAI lesson (or observation coupled with videotaping or audiotaping) can provide the design team with a wealth of information about the lesson and its appropriateness for the target population. You, or members

Examples of Pretest and Posttest Data for Instructional Objectives

	Instructional Objective	Evaluation Criteria	Average Pretest	Average Posttest	Revision Needed
1.1	Brainstorming list of topics	list 10 items	6	17	no
1.2	Freewriting on topic of choice	write for 5 mins.	3.6 mins.	5.3 mins.	no
1.3	Focused journal write on topic	write for 5 mins.	3.9 mins.	3.9 mins.	yes

Figure 7.4: Sample of Pretest and Posttest Data

of your team, can sit with users as they access and try out the lesson, record their questions, comments, behaviors, body language, frustrations, problems, and suggestions for improvement.

Who Should Be Involved in Field Testing?

Although you will probably be responsible for leading the field-testing effort, as the original author of the lesson and the composition specialist on your CAI team, a number of other people will also be involved. To encourage you to think about field-testing supporters, we have identified a few of these individuals below and briefly described the roles they might play. It is important, however, not to let this list limit the people you involve in field testing. We urge you, rather, to identify the field-testing schedule that will best fit your project and your schedule, and, only then, to decide which individuals will be needed to carry out this schedule.

Team Members

In addition to the composition specialist, other members of a CAI team will play important roles before, during, and after a lesson is being field tested. Before testing begins, they will help identify those components of the lesson that might benefit from close attention in a field-testing situation. The programmer, for example, might express a lingering dissatisfaction with the way the lesson currently stores and transfers student writing input in a file system. He or she might suggest that one or more field-testing situations require users (both teachers and students) to express their reactions to the storage and filing system. The educational specialist on the CAI team might identify very different concerns: whether, for instance, student users become confused at certain points in the lesson or whether the documentation for teachers is adequate.

By asking every member of a design team to identify potential trouble spots *before* testing begins, you can design a thorough and informative program of field testing. Team members can also be of help in planning, scheduling, and designing field-testing sessions; creating feedback forms (surveys, questionnaires, check sheets, etc.); identifying appropriate settings and subjects; and suggesting data-collection methods.

Team members can also be of help during and after the process of field testing. They can assist the composition specialist in conducting sessions with teachers or students, take notes on users' verbal responses to the lesson, videotape field-testing situations, interview users, and record the location of problem areas. After field-testing sessions have been conducted, team members can help make sense of the data they have collected. They can compile comments, count responses and present them in tabular or chart form, compare the data from various user groups, and make specific suggestions for revision.

Students

As the target audience for the lesson, students will provide most of the data collected during field-testing situations. They can be asked to give their general impression of a lesson or to respond to more focused questions in field-testing interviews. Students can fill out questionnaires or check sheets, think "aloud" while a team member audiotapes their running commentary on the lesson, or simply respond naturally to a lesson while a team member videotapes their problem-solving activities and body language.

As a group, students' performance on specific activities within a lesson can provide a design team with valuable data on the success of various instructional objectives. As individuals, students can provide data on the lesson's attractiveness, ease of use, apparent "friendliness," gaps, or biases.

Teachers

Whether a design team plans to market a CAI lesson widely or simply distribute it, gratis, to a few colleagues for use in their classes, field-testing data will need to be collected from other teachers. Colleagues can tell a design team how appropriate the lesson would be for the courses and the specific student populations they teach and what documentation they would need for the lesson to get it up and running on a particular brand or model of computer. They can define points of theoretical or pedagogical disagreement, identify gaps in the lesson's content, catch surface errors that have escaped earlier proofreading efforts, and discuss ways in which they can see the lesson being used within their writing classroom or writing program.

Administrators

Often, the decision to buy a particular piece of CAI software is made by a colleague who administers a writing program, an English department, or a writing lab. By consulting with these individuals during field testing, you can find out what things they consider attractive about your team's CAI lesson and what things they consider to be less than optimal. Questionnaires, surveys, or interviews with administrators can provide data on lesson content, pricing, technical support, and documentation for a CAI lesson.

After reviewing the material we have just presented on field-testing methods, you might want to take some time to design at least part of your own field-testing program. In figure 7.5, you can see how Jean might have designed a field test for a journal-writing activity within her freewriting lesson. We suggest you fill out a similar worksheet for each field test you plan to undertake.

As the example illustrates, Jean will survey a small sample of her target population to find out how they feel about writing journal entries on the computer in a writing lab. She will complete this field test while she is testing the effectiveness of several other instructional objectives in her lesson. At the end of this chapter, on Worksheet 25: Designing Field Tests, we have provided a worksheet, much like the one Jean completed, for designing the field tests you want to carry out on your own CAI lesson.

Finally, you will want to plan a systematic method of recording the results for each of the field tests. Field tests often produce so much data that you will have to summarize the results of each test in order to make them useful in your revision efforts. In figure 7.6, you can see how Jean might have filled out a summarizing worksheet for the field test she identified in the last activity.

As you can see, Jean's field test provided valuable information for use in revising her lesson. She wanted to determine whether students were bothered by composing journal entries on a computer in the writing lab. Students who took the survey did not mention being bothered by the electronic composing situation, but they did indicate that one journal-writing assignment out of five used for this activity was inappropriate. Because of these comments, Jean revised the

Example of Designing Field Tests

	Field Test # ___3___
Field-Test Question(s)	Are those writing activities connected with Instructional Objective 4.5 (write at least five journal entries each week, spending at least ten minutes on each entry) problematic in the public setting of the writing lab?
Field-Test Situation(s)	Observe whether students complete the journal writes according to Objective 4.5. Have students complete a survey that asks whether their journal-writing activities were constrained by the writing-lab setting.
Field-Test Sample(s)	6 students (3 male and 3 female) randomly selected from my Advanced Composition class.
Field-Test Method(s)	Pretests and posttests based on the evaluative criteria associated with Instructional Objective 4.5 (i.e., do they complete the entries?). Survey item asking students to describe how they feel about using computers in a semi-public place to complete journal writes (i.e., how do they *feel* about the entries?).
Notes	Field test all three Instructional Objectives I'm unsure about (4.3–4.5) during the same field-testing session, using the same sample. As students finish the field-testing session, give them a short survey and ask them questions about the writing strategies covered by the three objectives.

Figure 7.5: Sample of Worksheet 25 Activity

Example of Summarizing Field-Test Data

Summary of Field-Test Data	*Sample:* 6 students
	
	• Completed all journal entires: 5
	  Completed 4 journal entries: 1
	
	• Didn't like journal writing on computers in lab: 0
	  Liked journal writing on computers: 4
	  Didn't mind journal writing on computers: 2
	
	• Negative remarks about journal-writing assignment #3: 4
		Field Test # ___3___

Suggested Revisions	Revise journal-writing assignment #3	
Team Member in Charge	Jean	
Revisions Completed	4/30/86	

Figure 7.6: Sample of Worksheet 26 Activity

assignment in question. At the end of this chapter, we provide Worksheet 26: Summarizing Field-Test Data, on which you can summarize the data you collect during your own field tests.

Summary

The process of creating a CAI lesson has a great deal in common with the process of writing. The ultimate success of both are dependent on the author's willingness to revise and refine early versions of a product. The work you and your team have done thus far—planning the content of a CAI lesson, designing an appropriate pedagogical approach, writing an initial screen-by-screen lesson script, creating a program, and getting a version of the lesson running on a computer—is only the beginning of a long process of revision.

From experience, we know that successful revisions of a CAI lesson depend on a systematic and thorough program of field testing. Only such a program can test the lesson under realistic constraints—with real students, teachers, and administrators; in real classrooms; as a working part of a real writing program. In this chapter, we discussed some of the important questions connected with designing a field-testing program.

What lesson components should be field tested?

When should field testing take place?

How should field testing be undertaken?

Who should be involved in field testing?

At the end of this chapter we have provided a number of worksheets related to designing a program of field testing. We encourage you to adapt them as necessary for your own CAI lesson.

132   *Cynthia L. Selfe*

Worksheet 23: Identifying Field-Testing Questions

Before beginning the tasks identified below, work through the latest version of your team's CAI lesson on a computer, then respond to the tasks we have provided below.

1. Now that you have worked through the lesson, you can identify those instructional activities which need revision. Choose those activities that seemed confusing, overly difficult, boring, inappropriate, or unfinished. List the instructional objectives that would benefit from field testing in the space whe have provided below.

2. In the space that follows, list questions that you have about the lesson's attractiveness. Consider such things as the lesson's tone, the computer persona used in the instruction, screen design techniques, examples, writing activities, organization, length, etc.

3. In the space that follows, list those questions you have about the lesson's ease of use. Questions may resemble some of the following: Can a student in my class follow the directions I've provided for turning on the computer and accessing the lesson? Is the initial menu confusing? Are there additional places where "help" screens are needed? Is the screen text at an appropriate reading level?

4. In the space that follows, list those questions you have about how the lesson will fit into a writing classroom or program. You might, among other things, want to ask the following questions: How would a teacher use this lesson in a unit devoted to writing narratives? Would this lesson be appropriate as a homework assignment, or is it too long? Could the lesson be used by a student, without a tutor's aid, in our writing lab?

5. Use the following space to list any reservations you might have about the lesson's content. If possible, state these reservations in a question form, as in these examples:

Should the lesson include a discussion of ＿＿＿＿＿＿＿＿＿＿＿＿ ?

Is the concept of ＿＿＿＿＿＿＿＿＿＿ appropriate for my audience?

Have I discussed the concept of ＿＿＿＿＿＿＿＿＿＿ in a form my audience can understand?

Does the use of ＿＿＿＿＿＿＿＿ activities represent the most current information the profession has about writing, the writing process, and writing theory?

Worksheet 23 continued

6. In the space that follows, list any questions you might have about the biases reflected in this lesson and their impact on an audience. Consider cultural, economic, language, and gender biases among others.

7. In the space that follows list any other questions you have about this lesson that may best be answered in a field-testing situation.

Worksheet 24: Scheduling a Field-Testing Program

As the design team agrees on the field tests that should be completed in connection with your CAI lesson (Worksheet 25), schedule a field-testing program using this worksheet.

Field-Test Schedule   Page _____

Worksheet 25: Designing Field Tests

Complete this worksheet using the questions and concerns you identified on Worksheet 23: Identifying Field-Testing Questions.

Designing Field Tests

	Field Test # _____
Field-Test Question(s)	
Field-Test Situation(s)	
Field-Test Sample(s)	
Field-Test Method(s)	
Notes	

Worksheet 26: Summarizing Field-Test Data

After completing each field test for your CAI lesson, fill out this summarizing worksheet.

Summarizing Field-Test Data

	Field Test # _____
Summary of Field Test Data	
Suggested Revisions	
Team Member in Charge	
Revisions Completed	

8 SPREADING THE WORD ABOUT CAI SOFTWARE

For some authors, the long process of designing and producing a CAI lesson is complete when the first student sits down in front of a computer monitor and begins to work through a finished instructional unit. For other authors, the lengthy job of completing a lesson marks only the beginning of an even longer campaign to spread the word about CAI in general and their own lesson in particular. Some authors want to share their software with a few colleagues in their own English departments; others want to describe their lesson to large groups of teachers at professional conferences; still others hope to sell their software to publishing firms that provide national distribution.

This chapter is directed toward authors who want to reach a wider audience with their CAI lessons. Our discussion will touch on four suggestions.

1. Demonstrate CAI software locally.
2. Talk about CAI software at professional meetings.
3. Write about CAI software in professional publications.
4. Explore the possibility of publishing CAI software.

Demonstrate CAI Software Locally

One of the most effective ways of getting other teachers interested in a completed CAI lesson is to undertake a series of local demonstrations. Authors can demonstrate software for colleagues in their own English department, to teachers in other disciplines who teach writing-intensive courses, and to faculty from other institutions. These demonstrations can be given at faculty meetings held in the author's own school, presented at colloquia sponsored by local colleges or universities, shown as a part of regional curriculum workshops, or done as a component of summer writing projects.

In fact, the only problem with giving demonstrations is that they are too popular. Composition teachers of all sorts, working at all levels, are hungry for CAI lessons that are pedagogically and theoretically sound. Once an author demonstrates a successful CAI lesson to one or two local groups, the computer-user grapevine is activated, and requests begin to pile up.

To be effective, a demonstration requires practice, advanced planning, and organization. In the list below, we provide several things to think about during the planning of a demonstration.

Involvement

The optimal demonstration involves hands-on experience with a piece of CAI software. Some authors prefer to let teachers work through the lesson themselves while others feel that lessons are best demonstrated with students working and teachers watching. In either case, make sure that everyone in the audience can see what is going on. If more than a few people will attend, provide several machines or use a projection system that creates a display suitable for a large group. The more people actively engaged in a demonstration, the more successful it is likely to be.

Time

Unless a CAI lesson is short, consider demonstrating only part of it. Especially if the lesson involves lengthy writing activities, most teachers and students will not be able to complete the entire unit of instruction during a single sitting. For purposes of the demonstration, choose one or two representative activities from the lesson that last a total of fifteen to twenty minutes. In the introduction, be sure to identify which activities you have chosen for the demonstration, and discuss how these parts fit into the lesson as a whole.

Documentation

Work with your design team before the demonstration to write some descriptive documentation for your CAI lesson. Interested individuals will approach you after the presentation and ask for such materials. As part of this documentation, think about including a brief description of the lesson and its purpose, a list of the lesson's major instructional objectives, examples of the writing activities it incorporates, student comments about the lesson, suggestions about how the lesson can be incorporated in a writing classroom or program, and technical specifications for the computers on which the program can be run (models, memory constraints, programming language capabilities, graphics requirements, etc.). In addition, describe how interested parties can obtain a copy of the lesson and the cost of this service.

Questions

Save plenty of time for questions about the CAI lesson. During the first few demonstrations you give, record the queries and use them to shape your next presentation. Some authors prepare answers for a list of "frequently asked" questions about a CAI lesson and distribute them along with other documentation.

Equipment

If possible, use your own computer to demonstrate a CAI lesson. This piece of equipment is familiar, and you know that the lesson will run on it without a hitch. If you must use other computers for a demonstration, make sure they can accommodate your software and that you know how to work with them. Double- and triple-check hardware-software compatibility.

Practice

Computers are notorious for making teachers look bad in demonstration situations. If possible, schedule early practice sessions in the same room and with the same machines you will use during the demonstration. These dry runs will allow you time to track down extension cords, system disks, electrical power strips, and other necessities.

Talk about CAI at Professional Meetings

Professional conferences at the regional and national level are devoting increasing amounts of program time and exhibit space to teachers who are interested in computer-assisted writing instruction. Because these conferences attract a large number of teachers, they are perfect places to talk about CAI software.

Among the larger gatherings that encourage an exchange of information on computer-assisted language instruction are the annual meetings of the National Council of Teachers of English, the Conference on College Composition and Communication, the National Educational Computing Conference, and the International Reading Association. A host of other conferences—regional, national, and international—also provide forums for authors who want to share their CAI lessons. They include meetings like:

Microcomputers and the Learning Process (Clarkson College)

Computers and Writing

Microcomputers and Basic Skills in College (CUNY)

Computers and the Humanities

Writing for the Computer Industry

International Conference on Computers in the Humanities

Most of these gatherings accept papers or presentations about specific pieces of CAI software, and some provide time for demonstrations.

If you are going to demonstrate your CAI software at one of these gatherings, be sure to read the advice in the previous section about demonstrations. If you are going to talk about your CAI software at a professional meeting without demonstrating it, you might want to think about some of the following considerations:

Overview

In an oral presentation, it is hard for an audience to get a sense of the whole lesson as you and your design team created it. One way to overcome this difficulty is to show a visual map of the entire project. Figure 8.1, for instance, shows a visual map that Jean might have created for her freewriting lesson. If the audience can see such a map early in your talk, they have a much better chance of following the rest of your presentation. Also useful for overview purposes is a one-page description of the software's purpose, general philosophy, and hardware compatibility. The following paragraphs are a one-page description that might have been written by Jean for her freewriting lesson.

Example of One-Page Software Description

Title: Freewriting Lesson

Purpose

This lesson was designed to be used in conjunction with any writing-intensive course that includes the use of freewriting. It is designed to accomplish three main purposes: (1) to review standard lecture points about freewriting; (2) to describe the strategies of focused, automatic, and timed freewriting; and (3) to get students to practice freewriting strategies in a journal-writing setting.

Primary Objectives

After going through the instruction provided in this lesson, students will accomplish the following objectives: (1) write three practice freewrites, of at least twenty lines each, employing focused, automatic, and timed freewriting; (2) create at least five journal writes, spending at least ten minutes on each, using one of the three strategies of freewriting named above.

General Philosophy

This lesson is designed with three main assumptions in mind: (1) writing is one way to solve problems, (2) there are a number of different strategies for solving problems using writing, (3) freewriting strategies can be useful problem-solving heuristics.

Hardware Compatibility

The lesson will run on an IBM PC with 256K and DOS 3.0. Lesson disks are double-sided, double-density. The lesson code is written in UCSD Pascal.

Excerpts

One effective way to describe a piece of CAI software without demonstrating it is to show excerpts of a typical student's interaction with the program. These excerpts can be typed on a handout for the audience, shown on an overhead transparency, or included on photographic slides of actual instructional screens. The exchange that follows is a selection of excerpted student-computer dialogue from a CAI lesson on narratives that exists as part of the WordsWork series. Note that in this excerpt, the author has attempted to differentiate between the two parties involved in the dialogue—printing material produced by the computer in upper- and lower-case text while depicting the material produced by the student in upper case text only. Whatever method you choose, make sure that the excerpts can be seen and *read* by every member of the audience.

Example of an Excerpt from CAI Software

Okay, Therese, you've done short journal writes on three topics that you think might be suitable

Example of Visual Overview of a CAI Lesson

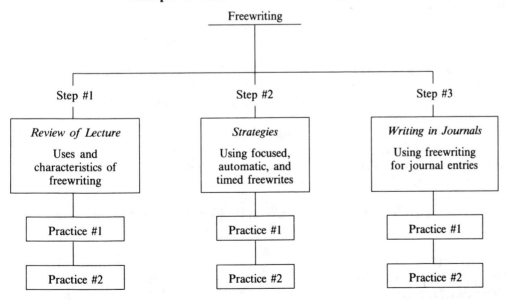

Figure 8.1: Sample of Visual Overview

for your narrative assignment—running away from home, the time I tried to tip my baby brother out of his crib and roll him down the stairs, and the time Don Bliss asked me out. With which of these topics do you want to continue? It might be the one you like best, the one about which you have the most to say, or the one you think will interest your audience the most. When I type *, you write in the topic you've chosen.

THE TIME DON BLISS ASKED ME OUT

Therese, I think that's a great choice. But let's try a focused journal write on that topic to make sure. I want you to take five minutes to tell me the story by typing it in on my screen. Remember, this is a freewrite, so you don't have to worry about grammar and spelling.

I really want to know what the major events of your narrative are and how you feel about what happened. Because this is your second journal write on this topic, you can begin to remember some detail, choose some location in which to set your story, and think of the point or message you are trying to get across to your reader by telling this story. I hope my directions are clear. Onward!! Remember, no more than five minutes!

LIKE I SAID BEFORE, I GUESS I WANT TO TALK ABOUT THE TIME I *THOUGHT* DON BLISS ASKED ME OUT. THE PROBLEM WAS THAT HE WAS ASKING ME FOR A FRIEND BUT I THOUGHT HE WAS ASKING FOR HIMSELF. THIS HAPPENED AT CHARLEVOIS HIGH SCHOOL WHERE I WENT TO SCHOOL. I WAS ABOUT 16 AND SO WAS DON. HE WAS REALLY A HUNK BUT HE NEVER PAID TOO MUCH ATTENTION TO ME AND I WAS TOO SHY TO LET HIM KNOW HOW I FELT. I KEPT FANTASIZING ABOUT US BUT THAT'S AS FAR AS IT WENT UNTIL ONE DAY AFTER CLASS WHEN HE ASKED ME IF I WAS GOING TO THE GAME AND I SAID NO. OF COURSE I THOUGHT HE WANTED TO TAKE ME BUT HE WAS ASKING FOR A FRIEND. I WAS SO STUPID THAT WHEN I FOUND OUT THE TRUTH I WAS TOO EMBARRASSED TO LET ON WHAT I HAD THOUGHT. I WANT TO LET OTHER GIRLS KNOW THAT THEY HAVE TO BE HONEST OR THEY'LL END UP IN THE SAME SITUATION. ALSO MAYBE I WANT TO TALK ABOUT HOW I THOUGHT DON BLISS WAS SO GREAT UNTIL I LEARNED BETTER. YOU CAN'T JUDGE A PERSON FROM HIS LOOKS. HE HAS TO BE HONEST ABOUT HIS FEELINGS TOO. IF EVERYONE WAS HONEST DATING WOULDN'T BE SO HARD IN HIGH SCHOOL.

Theory and Philosophy

In most professional meetings, the audience will be interested in knowing the theoretical and pedagogical philosophy that lies behind a piece of CAI software. Some authors prepare philosophical statements or bring copies of articles in professional publications that address these concerns. In any case, you should be prepared for questions on the theoretical foundations of your CAI software.

Availability

Come prepared to trade and sell your CAI. If your software is theoretically and pedagogically sound, teachers will want it. Before you come to a professional meeting, discuss with your team the best way of distributing your software. You might be content to barter or trade for lessons that other teachers create, but set up contingency plans for selling your software to individuals as well. Decide how much the software is going to cost and what the price includes (disk copying, compatibility support, continuing advice on product use, etc.). Draw up a short statement describing the terms of sale, and have a lawyer look at it.

Write about CAI Lessons in Professional Publications

With leaner budgets and increasing travel costs, it is not always possible to talk about CAI projects in person. Articles and reviews in professional journals provide one way of getting around this problem by distributing information about CAI software to larger audiences. Articles can serve not only to describe the purpose and structure of CAI software, but also to report empirical evidence of the lesson's effectiveness with a specific audience.

Some of the journals that publish articles on CAI and CAI software reviews are included in the following list.

> *Byte*
> *Collegiate Microcomputer*
> *Computers and the Humanities*

Computers and Composition

Creative Computing

Educational Technology

Journal of Computer-Based Instruction

Journal of Courseware Review

Perspectives in Computing

Writing Lab Newsletter

We suggest looking over back copies of these publications and requesting editorial information before writing or submitting an article about a particular piece of CAI software.

Information about software projects is also covered in the newsletters and information sheets published by educational/computer organizations around the country. Most of the timely publications put out by these groups offer software reviews and access to a valuable network of computer users across the country. Often, readers can find CAI available for barter or for the price of copying. Four of the larger organizations and appropriate contact persons are listed below. Ask other computer users in your own school or department for organizations operating on a local level.

National Council of Teachers of English
Assembly on Computers in English
Jack Jobst
Michigan Technological University
Houghton, MI 49931

Conduit
Molly Hepler
Oakdale Campus
Iowa City, IA 52240

English Microlab Registry
T. Barker
Texas Tech University
Lubbock, TX 79409

Minnesota Educational Computing Consortium
(MECC)
2520 Broadway Drive
St. Paul, MN 55113

When corresponding with these networking organizations, both on the national and local levels, it is best to include a stamped, self-addressed envelope for replies. Many of these groups operate on a lean budget that allows little room for unplanned mailing expenses.

Explore the Possibility of Publishing CAI Software

If you want maximum exposure for a piece of CAI software, exploring the possibility of distributing it through a publishing house or a software concern might be appropriate.

Most teachers have some contacts with representatives from the major educational publishing houses—Scott-Foresman; Houghton Mifflin; Little, Brown; Prentice-Hall; Wadsworth; Holt, Rinehart, and Winston; Allyn and Bacon; among others. All of these firms are testing the marketing waters in connection with CAI. Some have made preliminary explorations of publishing possibilities. Other firms are already involved. Houghton Mifflin, for example, publishes the Dolphin series and Little, Brown now markets Grammar Lab. There still exists among these firms, however, a general wariness about devoting resources to CAI projects. In general, this condition exists because traditional publishing concerns are set up to handle books, not computer products. The firms are not set up to handle research and development of CAI projects, to provide service for such projects after they are marketed, or even to gauge the success of these products as marketing ventures.

If you decide to approach one or more of these large publishing firms with a CAI product, be prepared to provide a prospectus for the project that describes the software's purpose, structure, packaging, organization and content, target audience, and competition.

Authors can also turn to software houses for publishing opportunities. Increasing numbers of such concerns are now distributing educational software for the writing classroom. Among them are:

Instructional/Communications Technology, Inc.

Krell Software Corp.

Queue, Inc.

Orange Cherry Media

American Educational Software

Unicorn Software Company

Micro Power & Light

Most of these companies list software in catalogs that they distribute and some cross-list software in directories put out by companies such as IBM, Apple, or Commodore. Software companies will also want to see a prospectus for a CAI project. Because some of these companies produce software for limited brands of computers, be ready to provide technical specifications about hardware compatibility.

Summary

CAI software that is pedagogically and theoretically sound may deserve distribution outside the author's own classroom or educational institution. To spread the word about a CAI package to other colleagues who use computers in their writing classrooms and programs, we have suggested four activities in this chapter.

Demonstrate CAI software locally.

Talk about CAI software at professional meetings.

Write about CAI software in professional publications.

Explore the possibility of publishing CAI software.

Activities like those we have listed above will have additional benefits as well. Through talking about CAI software to professional audiences, demonstrating software to teachers, and writing about CAI in professional publications, you will come in contact with a great network of teachers who have interests similar to yours and who can support your efforts to incorporate computers into writing classrooms and programs. These teachers will keep you informed about new technological developments in computer hardware and software; new methodological developments in writing-intensive, computer-assisted learning situations; and the new theoretical, philosophical, and ethical concerns that the introduction of computers may inspire.

Tapping into this network can also increase professional involvement at the local, regional, and national levels. Certainly, our profession's increasing use of computers in composition courses opens up exciting new vistas for research on writing and the teaching of writing. Similar opportunities exist for publishing about computer-assisted writing instruction, for serving on professional advisory councils which address the concerns of technology, and for establishing CAI-oriented programs at all levels.